Richard Goodwin was born in Persia in 1913 where his father was British Vice Consul. He was educated in the UK public school system, Haileybury College. His naval training was on the well-known training ship, *HMS Conway*, of the Royal Naval Reserve. Entering the Second World War as a navigator, Goodwin eventually served on top secret, highly classified mine sweeping operations during the war, on *HMS Borde* and *HMS Whitehaven*. He married Joan Gamon, during the war, whom he met in Chile while with the merchant marine, as a cadet, sailing between Liverpool, UK and Valparaiso, Chile. Goodwin participated in the invasion of Normandy in charge of landing crafts and was wounded on the beaches there. In December 1943 he was awarded the Distinguished Service Cross (DSC) for valor, among other medals. He was selected by the British Admiralty to travel to Central and South America as the British government's envoy to speak about the efforts of the Royal Navy in World War II. He later took on a post for marine operations in northern Peru with Lobitos Oilfields and later became the South America representative for W.R. Grace's shipping division, Grace Line, New York and Lykes Lines, New Orleans. He was transferred to Panama. He retired in Naples, FL, where he became the Court Interpreter for the City of Naples until age of 80. Commander Richard J. G. Goodwin died in Peru at the age of 99.

Dedicated in part to:

- **Hamish and Ella McMurray**—"a true guardian," helped on schooling. Launching naval career and counsel on many aspects of young adult life.

- **Captain of the *HMS Borde*, Roland Keith Hudson**, under whom Goodwin served, a proponent of everything good. A great naval officer, self-effacing and shy. If he did not have these traits, he would never have been chosen to command an experimental vessel such as the *Borde*.

Commander
Richard J. G. Goodwin

# A VIEW FROM THE MINESWEEPER'S BRIDGE

## A ROYAL NAVAL OFFICER'S WORLD WAR II MEMOIR

AUSTIN MACAULEY PUBLISHERS™

LONDON • CAMBRIDGE • NEW YORK • SHARJAH

**Ordering Information**
Quantity sales: Special discounts are available on quantity purchases by corporations, associations, and others. For details, contact the publisher at the address below.

**Publisher's Cataloging-in-Publication data**
Goodwin, Commander Richard J. G.
A View from the Minesweeper's Bridge

ISBN 9781647500443 (Paperback)
ISBN 9781647509033 (Hardback)
ISBN 9781647509040 (ePub e-book)

Library of Congress Control Number: 2020925232

www.austinmacauley.com/us

First Published (2021)
Austin Macauley Publishers LLC
40 Wall Street, 33rd Floor, Suite 3302
New York, NY 10005
USA

mail-usa@austinmacauley.com
+1 (646) 5125767

Many thanks to Lisa Akoury-Ross, my literary agent and publishing consultant, for her guidance and feedback, as well as editor, Kathleen A. Tracy for her ability to reshape our father's personal story without losing his voice as he recounted the inspiring and riveting story of his life. We also wish to thank the Imperial War Museum of UK for their permission to publish photos of the two British Navy ships, *HMS Borde*, and the *HMS Whitehaven* and John Shepherd of *liverpoolships.org* for his permission to publish the photo of *MV Reina del Pacifico*.

# Table of Contents

# Foreword

In the latter years of our father's life, around the age of 90, he was living for some time in Naples, Florida. Our mother had passed away seven years earlier in 1996. After her death, one of the ways he chose to pass the time was to spend hours pecking with one finger on a computer. He also often phoned my sister, Sylvia, for tips on how to trace his parents' genealogy. We were just glad he was finding something to occupy his time especially since distance separated us. Little did we know what subsequently would result. Five years later in Ottawa, Canada, with the family reunited there for his ninetieth birthday, we were quite surprised when he presented each of us a bound copy of a manuscript titled *My Memoirs.*

We three siblings—Sylvia, Clive, and I—each perused the 160 single-spaced pages interspersed with pictures, letters, and maps. At the time, with our own hectic lives, raising families, focusing on careers, and much more, we didn't pay much attention to it, and we each more or less relegated it to a shelf in our respective homes.

On July 28, 2012, at the age of 99, our father passed away in Lima, Peru. Some five years later, I was prompted to pick the memoir off the shelf and began reading it in earnest. I became absorbed by every page that transported me into an absolutely fascinating life and world of this man I called my father. Perhaps in his absence and at my stage in life, I saw it all with a totally new perspective. While I had been aware of his childhood in Persia, his naval escapades in World War II, and then his life in Peru, I was amazed and intrigued at the extraordinary details our father had cataloged in his memoir. The history, thoughtfulness, passion, humor, compassion, heroism, gallantry, discipline, duty, and love of our mother and family all came pouring off the pages.

I realized that the memoir was poorly compiled and full of typos—understandable considering his single-finger pecking on the computer. My wife, Lynda, urged me to retype the manuscript, and before I found the time, she began the process herself, exclaiming what an amazing record it was and that I should pay more attention to it. Soon we began jointly, and enthusiastically, retyping. I shared my profound awakening to this treasure with my sister and brother and that led to this story.

I gained an insight into and understanding of our father on a level I had not previously experienced. Yes, I knew he was a dashing, tall, good-looking man. He was a loving father and had a great sense of humor. He was interested in everything and could speak of many places around the world. He was fluent in French and Spanish. Growing up, we sensed he cared deeply about us all—first in Peru, then England, and later in the United States.

But it's fair to say I never really knew who he was deep down inside. Our father spoke very little about the past and shared only snippets about the war. He was never one to boast and kept a lot of personal feelings to himself. He rarely showed deep emotions outwardly. Some of that was due to his austere upbringing in a post-Victorian England. He was somewhat abandoned by his own parents and sent off to a grueling naval training. And of course, the proverbial British stiff upper lip and experience of World War II as a Royal Naval officer completed this picture.

I came away from his memoir with a new level of knowledge and understanding of why our father lived and behaved the way he did. I saw more vividly the deep and abiding love between my father and mother, which of course included their moments of turmoil and challenges. I was touched by the intense love they shared during the height of the war. I felt the full spectrum of the drama, sacrifice, risk-taking, inevitable fears of losing each other, and incredible glimpses into the gallantry of our father's role as a naval officer on the cutting edge of top-secret missions aboard minesweepers. Suddenly the war medals our father had given to me in a tarnished and tattered box at the end of his life took on a profound meaning. I now more fully comprehend what the Distinguished Service Cross among others represented and why they were bestowed on him by King George VI, his country, and the Royal Navy.

He concludes his memoir in a section called the Epilogue: "Yes, I think I have come pretty close to the end of my act on this stage, and I dedicate these few lines, not to an audience but to my fellow actors who have accompanied me so lovingly to this point—my family. Only they will find anything of interest in what I have written.

"The person who started the life is a game theory went on to say that it does not really matter who wins or who loses because the most important thing is how the game is played. I leave with you here some unsolicited testimonials as to how I have been judged by others who have accompanied me in the less pleasant stages of the game of life. I wonder if there is any life lived without some regrets. I hope I may be forgiven for presenting these testimonials with a little pride to compensate for those regrets."

Somehow, we three believe that more than just the family will find this story of interest, encouragement, and inspiration.

— Rodney, on behalf of my sister Sylvia
and my brother Clive

# Preface

The advent of computers and my retirement from regular employment arrived on the world scene almost in a dead heat. Perhaps it's the frightening capabilities of computers that was responsible for members of my family becoming interested in their ancestry and asking me about my past life. I tried to assure them—without any success—that they are descendants of a perfectly respectable British family. But a lack of family archives to back up that claim—photos, letters, scrapbooks—prompted my dear, suspicious relatives spending hours on the computer looking for any information to the contrary.

I do not know why my paternal grandfather, Benjamin Goodwin, and his wife, my granny, left no records as they passed through this world. Even more curious is why the only thing I know about my maternal grandparents is their last name: Grove. And even that may have been lost to time had I not been christened with that family name. In recent years, I've often wished I had the time to discover more about them than just a name.

That desire is what prompted me to embark on this memoir, to make certain that the same mystery will not surround me for the generations to come on my family tree.

I hope my efforts will spur all future Goodwins to also leave their descendants a written record of their life. And that they make it all about themselves, their story. That is what the people who follow will be most interested in reading.

— Richard John Grove Goodwin

# Chapter One
# My Parents

Gertrude Grove and Emery Goodwin, my parents, met in Worcestershire, England, sometime in 1906, around the time he went to work at the Imperial Bank of Persia's London head office. Founded in 1889 to establish a modern banking system in Persia, the British-owned Imperial Bank served as Persia's state bank, meaning it issued currency in the form of toman banknotes. The United States has dollars, Britain has pounds, and Persia had tomans.

If I may digress: It's been said by numismatists that the banknotes of the Imperial Bank of Persia are some of the most beautiful and largest ever issued for any nation. Unfortunately, very few specimens remain, nor did my father put any away for posterity.

The legal center for the bank was in London, but its activities were based in Tehran, with additional operations in other Middle Eastern countries. In 1907, my father was transferred to Persia, and the following year he and my mother were married at the British Consulate in Tehran. Photos from their wedding are formal—the ladies in their finest hats, everyone serious and unsmiling—giving them a rather impersonal air. My mother, holding a bouquet, looks almost somber while my father looks more relaxed. Several of the wedding party seem distracted by something off to their right. The two children in the photo—as well as a couple of adults—look like they'd really rather be anywhere but in front of the camera.

My father was later named the manager of the bank branch in Qazvin, located about two hours northwest of Tehran. He was also the British Consul there. Qazvin is a cultural center best known for its baklava, carpets, poets, and calligraphy museum. It is also where I was born in 1913. My mother had returned to England for my sister Kathleen's birth two years earlier then brought her back to Qazvin when she was just a few months old. Back then, travel between England and Persia was an excursion, a combination of train and ship that took considerable time and expense. That could be why I was born in Persia.

Growing up abroad meant I had little contact with my grandparents or other relatives. I know very little about my mother's family. I do know she was one of six children and that she and her siblings—Alice, Nelly, Kitty, Percy, and Harry—grew up on a farm near the border of Worcestershire and Shropshire, two counties in western England, an area known as the Midlands.

My father and his brother Harry were the only children of Benjamin Goodwin, a building contractor who lived all his life in Worcester at 100 Ombersley Road. He also had properties in Ladywood, which is a neighborhood in Birmingham, and in the Malvern Hills at British Camp, which is an Iron Age fort located at the top of Herefordshire Beacon. The fort, now a designated ancient monument, dates back to the second century BC and was once the site of a Norman castle. Going there is a step back in time.

My paternal grandparents were already in their eighties when I first visited the house in Worcester with my parents. Some of my most vivid childhood memories are of school holidays spent variously at those three places. On one occasion when I was about ten years old, my sister and I visited without our parents and were met at the railway station by my grandparents' chauffeur. He led us outside the depot to Granny's car, a luxury French model called a Delage. It was a large sedan—then called a saloon car—decorated with figures of cherubim and seraphim. I was impressed that Grandpa also had a Sunbeam touring car, green with white tires. I can still see him dressed in a long, white coat wearing a cap and goggles during the only occasion I rode in it.

My uncle Harry, a postal worker, lived only about three blocks from his parents. He and his wife Edith were parents to just one son, also named Harry, who as an adult would be a life insurance broker in London.

# Chapter Two
# Memories of Persia

The Persia of my childhood was not the Iran of today.

Prior to 1935, the country now called Iran and its surrounding areas was known as Persia, an ancient kingdom and ethnic group. Just as Britain is not the same thing as England, Iran is not the same thing as Persia.

The country of Iran was formed over the center of the ancient Persian empire, so people who identify as Persian make up the majority of the population. But there are also many other ethnic and tribal groups, such as Azeris and Kurds. So while all citizens of Iran are Iranians, only some are Persian.

In 1906, Persia was made a constitutional monarchy, its leader called a *shah*. After entrepreneur William Knox D'Arcy, who later founded British Petroleum, discovered oil in Persia in 1908, Great Britain and Russia vied to establish their political and diplomatic influence over the country and the shah, the latest chapter in what historians have dubbed The Great Game that had been going on for more than 50 years by then. Although the two countries were allies, Russia wanted to keep Britain from making commercial and military inroads into Central Asia, and the

UK didn't want Russia undermining it in India—Britain's jewel in the crown—in an effort to make it one of their satellites. In today's parlance, Persia became ground zero for those competing tensions. But it was also a beacon for foreign nationals, drawn by the possibilities provided by new oil money, which made the Imperial Bank of Persia all the more important.

I spent the first six years of my life in Persia and have absolutely no memories of my parents. Photos from that time show me as a reserved, fair-haired child whose resemblance to his mother increased as he got older. Most of the photos are posed rather than snapshots so it's hard to glean personality although my sister and mother generally look more vibrant and good-natured than me.

I do remember having a Persian nanny who looked after me. I have clear memories of my bedroom at Qazvin because a robber once entered it. We lived in a compound connected to my father's bank and afterward there were Cossack guards stationed outside my bedroom.

The sad part is that these memories cannot be checked by anyone who was around at that time in my life. I now find it incredible that I never asked my parents during my adult life if these were factual events or figments of my imagination.

During World War I, which started in 1914, Persia was occupied by British, Ottoman, and Russian forces but the country essentially remained neutral. Family photographs show how our lives were dominated by a military presence during the Great War. General Lionel Dunsterville was in command of the British garrison stationed in Qazvin, and Kathleen and I got into a lot of photographs with the soldiers. Even if you didn't know where the photos were taken, the era is evident by both the uniforms of the soldiers and the trim mustaches that were the style of the day, giving members of the garrison a dashing and adventurous appearance. I can't help but wonder if my childhood exposure to the military and their inherent derring-do indelibly imprinted on me a desire to one day follow in their honorable footsteps.

There was no question of any of us leaving Persia until the war was over. Then came the terrible influenza epidemic of 1918 that created so much havoc all over the world—as if the war itself had not already done that—killing more than 50 million people. Some estimates put the number closer to 100 million. The flu easily killed more soldiers than the war.

The reason for that rather large window is because neither the Axis nor the Allied forces reported information on the flu because it was considered top secret. Neither side wanted the other to know exactly how much the flu had weakened their military capabilities. Spain was a neutral country during World War I, so the medical community and press were free to publish information about the flu, so most of what we knew about the flu in Europe came from Spain. That is why the 1918 pandemic became known as the Spanish flu, even though it did not originate in that country. It just shows how in wartime priorities are upended. Everything, including public health issues, is seen through the prism of the need for military victory.

My most durable memories of life in Persia as a child are smells, which are almost impossible to describe. They are all to be my own personal memories, never to be shared with anyone who never played with me floating sticks down the irrigation ditches in fields of Persian clover. Every now and then in later years, I would catch a fleeting whiff that stirred my recollections of those early days, just as sometimes the light of the sun at certain times of day in certain places takes me back to an afternoon in Qazvin or Tehran. But there is just no way that those memory bursts can be described.

I have more memories of Tehran than Qazvin because that's where we were living before leaving Persia in 1919 when I was six. We had two dogs, but I don't recall their names. I remember being outside walking with my sister and our nanny one afternoon when a whirlwind literally lifted Kathleen off the ground. I recall how ill-tempered I was when awoken from my afternoon nap. I recall nothing of any education, although I understand that we had some. What a poor harvest of memorabilia! However, it's fortunate that our lives in Persia were so well-recorded by photographs.

# Chapter Three
# Crabtree Furlong

After defeating Napoleon in 1815, Britain was firmly established with France, Russia, Ottoman Turkey, and China as one of the world's great imperial powers. And Lord Nelson's victory over the French at Trafalgar in 1805 cemented Britain's global supremacy at sea. The British empire consisted of Canada and the four Maritime Provinces, South Africa, Australia, India, and the Caribbean. It was the control of world shipping that enabled the United Kingdom to bind the countries in the empire so effectively. Clearly, the empire needed a well-prepared supply of personnel trained in all aspects of government, finance, and commerce to protect it. That is how Crabtree Furlong Boarding School came to exist.

Looking more like a countryside weekend cottage than an educational institution, the school was run by Charlotte Hogg, known as Aunt Lotty to her students. My understanding is that Charlotte, who was unmarried, started the school so the children of her siblings—who all established careers in China—would get a good education. Among the students was her nephew Edward Hogg, who became a Royal Marine Captain during World War II.

Word of Crabtree Furlong spread virally among working parents, especially those based overseas, and that is how Kathleen and I ended up attending boarding school in the little village of Haddenham in Buckinghamshire. I don't recall saying goodbye to my mother before she returned to Persia. I think it says much for Aunt Lotty and her organization that Kathleen and I settled down so quickly and painlessly in her care.

I was about six when we were left at Aunt Lotty's. The ages of the other children ranged from 6 to 9 years old, and there were as many boys as girls. There were only about ten other students our age, so we all had the same teacher, Miss Britten. The boarding school's mandate was to ready its students for preparatory schools, which provided education for ages nine to the early teens. In addition to the basic reading, writing, and mathematics, we were taught French grammar by Miss Britten and conversational French by two very nice *madames* from Paris who stayed at the school each summer. During those two months, we could only speak French when in the presence of Mmes. Gaspard and Tabouret.

Education at Crabtree Furlong wasn't limited to academics. Aunt Lotty placed great emphasis on social graces. Everyone took dancing lessons twice a week, and she provided piano and violin lessons for those who showed the aptitude. Aunt Lotty was also an avid card player and taught everybody how to play bridge and whist; not just as a fun way to pass the time but to prepare us for a full life. Aunt Lotty and her staff taught us what the world outside of Crabtree Furlong would expect of us intellectually, socially, and personally in terms of general good behavior. I still marvel at how farsighted she was.

Aunt Lotty was both teacher and caregiver. She made arrangements to keep any students who couldn't go home during school holidays because their relatives could not have them for whatever reason. During the Easter holiday, she would arrange accommodation for all comers at Woolacombe, a seaside resort on the southwestern coast in North Devon with three miles of sandy beach on the Atlantic. So there we were, together with friends under the same roof, feeling safe and secure. What would we all have done without her? And those times together perpetuated literal lifelong friendships. When Kathleen was in her eighties, she was still in contact with two of Aunt Lotty's nieces who she befriended in 1920.

I can also bear personal witness that affairs of the heart also blossomed at Crabtree Furlong between boys and girls. In 1922, I met Patricia Nelson there. Like mine, her father also worked in Persia but not in the banking industry. I lost my heart—or a good part of it—to her, and our friendship lasted until 1933 when I made my first trip to sea. I heard that she got married before World War II broke out in 1939 and went to live in Malaysia until her family had to flee before the Japanese invasion.

After leaving Crabtree Furlong, most of the girls, including Kathleen, attended St. Swithin's, a boarding school in the southern England town of Winchester, which was founded in 70 AD as a Roman outpost, *Venta Belgarum*. It is known for its cathedral, one of the largest in Europe, and as the place where famed novelist Jane Austen died from mysterious causes. The boys were more dispersed, and I ended up at Norfolk House at Beaconsfield.

# Chapter Four
# Preparatory School

The next step up the ladder to a complete education for the sons of gentlemen was a preparatory school, and there were thousands of them in the British Isles back then. When I was nine, I left Crabtree Furlong for Norfolk House in Beaconsfield, Buckinghamshire, just outside of London. It was run privately by a graduate of Oxford University. Mr. H.E. Forrester was married to a lady who was as active in the running of the school as any lady could have been. On reflection, she was probably more active than most headmasters' wives in prep schools those days because she had no children of her own. Mr. and Mrs. Forrester were great people who certainly did their very best to educate and prepare us to enter a public school.

Norfolk House was a true-blue establishment. By that, I don't mean the American definition of being loyal. In early twentieth-century England, like today, the main political parties were Conservative, Labour, and Liberal. The color associated with Conservatives was and still is blue. The Labour Party was red, and Liberals were some unimportant color I never knew (Actually, it's yellow). Anyone who spoke proper English, whose father was employed in big business, who had been to school as a boarder at a prep school, public school, and either Oxford or Cambridge was considered to be true-blue. At a true-blue school, you would play cricket in summer and rugby in winter.

It is interesting how color can come to represent an ideology. When I was growing up, Russians and all communists were called reds, so as young boys, my classmates and I were brought up to believe that the Labour Party wielded a foreign and dangerous influence. At Norfolk House, the education dispensed was heavily blue, and I became a devotee until I grew up and expanded my political horizons.

While at Norfolk House, Persia was a world away. I didn't think much about it or how my parents were faring, until the morning Mr. Forrester called me into his study and related a fearsome experience my mother and father had endured. While traveling through the country, they were attacked by road bandits who killed their Persian driver, took all their belongings and valuables, then led my parents into the nearby desolate hills and held them captive. After assaulting my father, the bandits eventually left and disappeared into the desert landscape.

I never heard how exactly my parents were rescued, just that they somehow got word to someone in Tehran, and a rescue party was organized. I later found out that the bandits did not get everything. My mother had successfully hidden her engagement ring; it was the only item not stolen.

I was sorry when it was time to leave Norfolk House for a public school. In America and other countries, the term public school means that it is paid for by the government. Not so in England. The term public, which was first adopted by Eton, indicated it was a school open to the general public as opposed to a religious school that was only available to members of a certain church.

That said, *public* was defined rather narrowly since these schools have always been highly academically selective and pupils usually need to pass various tests for admission, not to mention have a family wealthy enough to afford the considerable tuition and room and board fees. So while public school might technically be open to anyone, they ended up being exclusive to a very small segment of the public. Today, most now allow day pupils, and many are co-ed in part or full. But traditionally and when I attended, they were boarding schools for boys 13–18.

Students moving on from prep school had to take and pass the Common Entrance Examination. I remember feeling very positive after taking the test because the questions did not seem difficult. And my optimism was rewarded because I did receive high marks. So high, in fact, that I was entered in the middle school at Haileybury rather than to the lower school.

I was to regret that.

# Chapter Five
# Higher Education

I started at Haileybury in September 1927. The school had quite a history. In October 1805, the directors of the infamous East India Company bought Haileybury House and the 60-acre estate it sat on to build a college specifically to educate civil servants to work in India and "qualify them for governing themselves."

Half a century later, the sheen was off the East India Company, which many thought had simply become too powerful, and the college would be a victim of changing attitudes against patronage. The public felt that all students graduating from British universities should have an equal opportunity to serve in India, not just those channeled through the East India Company's own college. So in the summer of 1855, Parliament passed legislation that essentially said the company couldn't run the school anymore and the college closed in 1858. Four years later, a new Haileybury College opened as an independent public school.

As the school system evolved, so too did education. In the days of Henry VIII, large commercial companies offered free education to any boy with the right qualifications so after school, he could work in that particular company or industry. Later through public schools, education enabled students to choose their own careers. By the time I came along, the best public schools had rather high standards.

My parents were abroad when I had started at Norfolk, a time when I would have dearly benefitted to discuss my future with them. If nine years old seems rather young to do any serious career planning for the rest of one's lifetime, such was our school system. I had always thought I'd like to take up seafaring, but by 14 years of age, it was already too late. I hadn't realized that to make it in the Royal Navy, I should have gone to Dartmouth Naval College—assuming my father could afford the expenses that serious training for the navy required. It was my failure to do well at Haileybury that made me give serious thought to the whole matter of my future.

I was bewildered by the difference in size between Norfolk House and Haileybury. My prep school had provided a relatively sheltered existence, with just 35 boys compared with the 400 boys at Haileybury. And it was very clear to me the day I entered Haileybury that some important chunk of my education was missing. It was probably in the lower school because I soon found that I was out of my depth with the middle school class level.

I fully realize now that the line of least resistance is a poor choice when problems have to be solved. I wish I could have explained my problem to someone at Haileybury rather than do nothing about it. I realize now how welcome a word of advice from my housemaster at Haileybury would have been. He had only about 40 boys under his supervision, but I felt that I had a poor chance of being given the solution I would have welcomed: to be put back into the lower school before my first term was over. As it was, I was left to wallow in the wake of students who had indeed started at the beginning instead of halfway into their college years.

While at Haileybury, Uncle Hamish and Aunt Ella (McMurray) came to play an important part in my life. Hamish was born in Galloway, Scotland, the son of a farmer. After finishing school, he applied for a post in the Imperial Bank of Persia in London in 1897. Three years later, he was sent to Persia where he served in several branches before being assigned to open the branch in Hamadan, where he was my father's boss but also became his friend.

From 1917 to 1918, Hamish led the bank's expenditure control commission, which financed Russian forces in Persia. Britain's Foreign Office assigned the Imperial Bank of Persia the delicate duty of maintaining good relations with both the Persian and Russian governments. The procedure which Hamish adopted over those two years earned him the Commander of the Order of the British Empire (CBE), which is awarded for outstanding work in your respective field. Aunt Ella was awarded an Order of the British Empire (OBE), which is given for achievement in the arts or sciences, public service, or charitable activities.

Hamish was appointed chief manager of the bank in 1920 but resigned in 1925 after developing a duodenal ulcer. I recall meeting with Hamish and Ella that year in England because my mother and father were home on leave, and Kathleen and I were on school holidays. After a successful ulcer operation, Hamish was elected to the board of the bank in London. In 1928, he was elected director, a position he held until he died.

Uncle Hamish and Aunt Ella, those dear people, took me into their household. They lived in a beautiful house in Surrey, and I spent many happy weeks there during school vacations from Haileybury. They had no children of their own and welcomed me as a son. Hamish became a true guardian for me where my schooling was concerned. He was aware of the poor progress I was making at Haileybury and my interest in the navy. When Dartmouth was ruled out because of my age, he pulled some very useful strings for me to get on the *HMS Conway*, a training ship for the Royal Naval Reserve, Britain's volunteer reserve force of the Royal Navy. I was a year too old, but that was overlooked, so in 1930, I left Haileybury and started my seafaring training. I'm sure that throughout my education at Norfolk House, Haileybury, and aboard the *HMS Conway*, my parents were kept informed of incidents as they occurred even if I never talked to them.

It was strange how everything seemed to have meaning the moment I joined the *HMS Conway*, which was anchored in the River Mersey. Obviously, the surroundings, the education subjects, and the duties inspired me. I now felt there was an incentive for everything I did and a belief that I would eventually become a Royal Naval Reserve officer, which required annual service on warships. But the bulk of the time after graduation from the *HMS Conway* would be in the Merchant Marines where you advanced by taking Board of Trade examinations for second officer, chief officer, and master. Instead of the aimlessness overwhelming me at Haileybury, I now felt that everything I learned from now on was directly aimed at achieving a career.

Education aboard the *HMS Conway* was considerably different than at Haileybury. All facets of seamanship were taught, and practical experience of boat handling became one of my favorite activities. Once we reached cadet captain status, we had to handle motor launches to and from the Rock Ferry pier during both during the day and at nighttime if necessary. We learned navigation as well as engineering and science, all to prepare us for the subsequent Board of Trade examinations we'd take after completing two years of service at sea.

My two years aboard *Conway* seemed to pass like a flash. I passed with an extra certificate, and Aunt Ella and Uncle Hamish came up from London for the graduation. Sadly, shortly after they returned home, Aunt Ella had a stroke, and she died a few hours later. She was a great godmother to me. But I had little time to grieve. I was ready to start my two years of required service working for a shipping company, the prerequisite for taking the second officer exam. And once again, Uncle Hamish interceded on my behalf.

# Chapter Six
# MV Laguna

Uncle Hamish helped me obtain an interview at the Pacific Steam Navigation Company (PSNC). The office was in Liverpool, and I was to be interviewed by Captain Kelly, the marine superintendent, for a two-year apprenticeship. I recall the occasion well because it gave me insight into the type of individual I was likely to meet and who I needed to convince that not only was I a fit and capable cadet now but would be equally qualified as a future officer for the shipping line.

The interview was timed for 1 pm; I arrived ten minutes early. I knocked, and a porter opened the door to reveal an elderly, sour-faced man who glanced at a wall clock.

"One o'clock?" he asked, his manner gruff. Then almost immediately, he said in the same gruff way, "Oh, come on in. Sit down."

I complied while the porter beat a hasty retreat. A few moments later, Captain Kelly got up, took his bowler off the hat stand, and disappeared, closing the door behind him. I imagined that he had gone out to lunch because he certainly would not need his hat in the restroom. Since he had not invited me to join him, I just sat and waited. Ten minutes passed, and he finally returned, hung up his hat, and sat down.

After perusing a file for a minute, he said, "Stand up, turn round, sit down," which I did in the order stated. Then he said, "Well I see you have a head, two arms, and two legs. That's all I need. Here, take these papers down to Mr. Greene."

Interview ended.

Needless to say, the interview with Captain Kelly of the PSNC left me depressed. I suspected that the file had contained the letter of recommendation Hamish had asked the former commodore of the PSNC—and his distant relative—to write. Captain Kelly's behavior was typical of someone who has to do something they have no control over. Namely, giving his blessing to my employment. All Captain Kelly did in the interview was approve my apprenticeship for a two-year period that my father would have to pay 100 pounds sterling for. However, there was no doubt that anyone looking for employment as an officer in the Merchant Marine would have to receive the blessing of a marine superintendent somewhere.

The world's dire economic situation in 1932 created a jungle for any young person—myself included—starting off on a career. It had begun on October 24, 1929, with a four-day collapse of stock prices that culminated with the stock market crashing on October 29. Black Tuesday, losing $30 billion in market value—the equivalent of $396 billion today, which was more than the total cost of World War I. That directly led to the Great Depression, the worst global economic disaster in history to date. Banks stopped lending, causing untold bankruptcies in the United States and abroad, bringing about devastating unemployment. In 1932, there were 12 million people jobless in the US, 5.6 million in Germany, and 2.7 million in the UK. New York City newspapers were filled with photographs of starving people forming so-called bread lines to get government-supplied food, mostly bread and soup. I remember boys in the *HMS Conway* having to leave because their parents could no longer pay the fees.

In that context, I should have been grateful for the recommendation letter that urged the PSNC to take me on as an apprentice despite Captain Kelly's snarkiness. Was possessing the correct number of limbs sufficient for me to move to the head of the line of 2.7 million unemployed? Couldn't they have found someone to recommend them, or didn't they want that kind of job? Or didn't they have the 100 pounds? I thought surely things had to get better while I was learning all I needed to know about all things nautical.

Hamish and I traveled to the Port of Hull in Yorkshire, where I picked up all the necessary uniforms and equipment my pending duty required. It was also where the *MV* (motor vessel) *Laguna* was docked. There, I met Captain Robert E. Dunn OBE and the chief officer, Mr. Patterson. They both lived at Hull as did most of the crew as I found out later. There were three other cadets who had already joined. We four shared a cabin with four bunks—two up and two down. I can now remember the name of only one of my cabin mates.

As soon as Hamish had left, I was instructed to change into my working clothes and join the other cadets at work. We sailed the next day for our coastwise calls at Glasgow and Liverpool where we completed our loading operations and then sailed to the Panama Canal. From there, we called at Guayaquil in Ecuador, ports in Peru, and four ports in Chile where we discharged the last of our outward cargo and started to load copper bars, lead bars, bagged sugar, and cotton for the UK and continental European ports.

When I joined, the *MV Laguna* was the newest of the PSNC cargo vessels. Built in 1923, she had twin screws, each operated by a diesel motor which exhausted out through pipes in the squat stack just aft of the bridge and almost level with it. The sounds of starting each of the two motors were heralded by a loud hiss of compressed air being injected into the cylinders followed by—if all went well— the first cylinders firing and the first exhaust ejection. As the motors started, their panting was very audible on the bridge, just as a diesel truck driver can hear the throb of the engine's exhaust. Only here on the *MV Laguna*, the cylinders down in the engine room were very much larger than those of a truck and consequently much, much louder. By comparison, marine steam propulsion engines were largely silent.

I mention these diesel motor idiosyncrasies because I had never imagined how so clearly aware the person handling the vessel in restricted areas should be of exactly when the engine orders are obeyed. Since all the ships of the PSNC cargo fleet were fitted with diesel engines, I considered ship handling one of the most important aspects of all the duties I was now trying to learn, especially how much of a delay should be allowed for the engineers below to obey an order during any maneuver. When I was on the bridge as the vessel was approaching a berth to dock or leaving a berth, seeing the answer to that question first-hand became an obsession for me. The sequence of *engine order > compressed air > first exhaust gasp > vibration of vessel* was all clearly noticeable on motor vessels and enabled me to learn without the intervention of a teacher.

That was just as well because my cadet apprenticeship experience during those early days was limited to washing down paintwork and painting it, washing down varnish and putting it on, chipping steel decks and applying red lead, and watching to make sure the stevedores actually stowed all the cargo as per the book and didn't pilfer any of it. The only duty that provided useful experience was doing shifts at the helm of the vessel. Since the cadets were unpaid, we were called to this duty to save the company from having to pay overtime to the hired sailors. But we had no coaching in the art of navigation during those early days of apprenticeship.

Captain Dunn was one of the heaviest smokers I had ever met but never carried cigarettes on his person. Every time he needed to smoke while he was on the bridge, he sent a cadet to his cabin to get one. I was told by my more experienced companions that the rule was to take one for yourself if you're not on watch, but I had no proof that was adhered to.

Captain Dunn was also one of the largest men I have ever met. He stood about 6'4" and weighed about 320 lbs. His decoration resulted from his activities as navigator (second officer) on one of the PSNC passenger vessels that escaped from a German battleship just before the Battle of the Falkland Islands in 1917, which he accomplished by his knowledge of the Straits of Magellan.

Chief Officer Patterson was about 50 years old, and the captain dominated him in every way. Together, they led what was a formidable group of Yorkshire inhabitants at the Port of Hull. They as well as the *MV Laguna's* carpenter and chief steward lived in the same area. They had apparently all been shipmates for some time.

During my time aboard the *MV Laguna*, only two incidents occurred that stand out in my memory as being unusual.

I shared my bunk with a cadet named Henwood, who was on the lower bed. He was from North Wales. I was never very friendly with him, and on one occasion, our association became physical. His drawer under our two bunks was on top of mine. One afternoon, he opened his drawer and left it open for a period of time I considered to be excessive because he was not taking anything out of it or putting anything away.

I closed it, and as I stood, I received a sharp blow to my chin. When I regained consciousness, I was lying on the settee being given water by one of the other cadets who had witnessed what I considered unprovoked aggression. Nothing further came of the matter because as far as I could foresee, retaliation was what my assailant was asking for, and I had no intention of satisfying him.

*MV Laguna* started her third voyage from the Port of Glasgow, and her crew of seamen was all native to that part of Scotland. They were a tough lot indeed, but we cadets never had much to do with them other than to work alongside them when we were chipping rust off the decks. This voyage took us down the east coast of South America to the Argentine port of Ingeniero White where we were to load bagged wheat for Callao in Peru. While we were there, I went ashore with one of the other cadets to attend a whist card party drive at the local officers' club, which wasn't over until about 11 pm. On my way back to the ship, I was walking down a seamy street lined with souvenir shops and bars when I came across a man lying on the sidewalk, mumbling. He had obviously been thrown out of the bar and was in such a sorry state of inebriation, I felt compelled to stop. As I bent over him, I recognized his face. It was Montgomery—Monty for short—one of our Glasgow seamen.

I asked if he was hurt but received no response. When I tried to move him, Monty opened his eyes and looked at me for a few seconds.

"Is that you, Lofty?" he asked, calling me by the nickname given me aboard because of my height.

I was relieved that my friend was not badly injured and helped him get up, which took considerable effort. With one of his arms draped around my neck, we started back to the ship. As we walked, he muttered obscenities over how he'd been treated at the bar then expressed gratitude for my help, all in his very distinctive Scotch accent. Every now and then we would stop, and he would mumble something about the ship and his friends aboard. And then he suddenly mentioned Henwood, the cadet who had clocked me on the chin.

I interpreted Monty's stated dislike of Henwood was intended to accentuate his gratitude toward me. As we were finally staggering up the gangway to the *Laguna*, Monty was very audible about how Henwood had attacked me while my back was turned. I told the gangway watchman that I would relieve him if he would see Monty back to his quarters. When he returned and reported that Monty was in his bunk, I was very happy to go to mine.

I found that my three companions were still ashore, so before climbing into my bunk, I left the door of our cabin ajar so that the light shone in from the passage outside. Getting into my bunk, I marveled at how Monty could get such a violent fixation regarding anything as insignificant as my run-in with Henwood. I was just about to welcome sleep when suddenly I heard the door open and saw Monty standing there with his arm raised, hand holding a knife, and muttering Henwood's name.

I leaped out of my bunk and confronted Monty. When he saw me, he dropped his arm and made no effort to resist my desperate grab for the knife. I led him out onto the deck and once again called the watchman. I kept the knife until the next day. I managed to prevent Henwood from finding out; the only other person who knew about the incident was the second officer I reported it to.

# Chapter Seven
# RMMV Reina Del Pacifico

I would soon learn that life on board this new vessel from builders Harland and Wolf was very different from my time on the *Laguna*. When the *RMMV Reina del Pacifico,* or *RDP* as she was referred to, launched on September 23, 1930, she was the world's most powerful and fastest diesel vessel as well as the most luxurious passenger liner trading to South America. The *RDP* carried 400 passengers in three classes, and her operating speed was 18 knots. Her old sister ships—the PSNC's *Oropesa, Orcoma,* and *Orbita*—could only accommodate about 150 passengers in first class and could only do 15 knots. Their days were numbered. The *RDP* came into service during a time of fierce competition for the passenger trade from Europe to South America, with companies such as Italy's Flotta Lauro and the Netherland's Nedloyd also launching fast, new ships.

The cadets' accommodations on the *RDP* were under the bridge in the same area as those of the captain and other deck officers. Three cadets kept watch on the bridge, one with each officer. The fourth cadet was on day work. 8 am–noon, and 1 pm–5 pm. His duties could be anything appropriate with any cleaning being done not in the view of passengers. The chief officer allocated those duties.

Unlike life aboard the freighters, there were some luxuries cadets could enjoy such as a hot soup break at 11 am in cold weather and an ice cream break in hot weather. But only in the second class. When off duty, the cadets were allowed very reasonable latitude to mix with passengers in second class, where we also had a table in the dining room. (The officers had the same latitude where first-class passengers were concerned.) The bar and passenger cabins were out of bounds, and we had to be off the deck and out of the passengers' sight by 10 pm.

In the two years that I was aboard the *RDP*, I did just about every job available. One of the more unusual was changing the clocks to show the correct local time, which corresponds to the vessel's current longitude. The most convenient time for gradually changing clocks is at night, so the passengers and crew know what time it is when they awake. It was the cadet on the middle watch at nighttime whose job was to change the time on each clock in every public room. The changes were made to each clock by applying the two terminals of a flashlight battery to the corresponding terminals on each clock.

I started the task at about 1 am each morning, and it took about an hour. The silence combined with the knowledge that I was in the immediate presence of so many people had a strange effect on me. I felt at peace in a way I find hard to explain. My travels around the passenger accommodations always included a stop at the night watch steward. Aboard ship, the steward is in charge of organizing and preparing food. There can be cabin stewards too, whose main job is to take care of the passengers' cabin rooms. The night watch steward on the *RDP* always had some of the most delicious appetizers available all night for any passenger who called for cabin service.

The *RDP* offered a veritable academy for learning about seafaring in general and navigation of seamanship in particular compared with what the freighters had to offer cadets. The vessel was fitted with all the instruments and facilities for modern navigation. One of the navigation improvements on board this ship was the Chernikeeff Log, which was an underwater device, usually retractable, used to measure speed and distance. It was invented by an officer of the Russian Imperial Navy and further developed by the British Navy. Before the advent of this device, the distance that a vessel has traveled between any two points on the map had to be measured by a brass propeller attached to a plaited cord that was towed behind the ship. As the propeller rotated in the water, the cord twisted, turning a clock specially constructed and calibrated to convert the revolutions to nautical miles. Total miles on the clock divided by the time between readings gave average speed and total distance run since the last reading. Obviously, this method, called Taffrail Logs, was inexact.

The Chernikeeff Log replaced the propeller method. It used a four-bladed propeller at the end of a brass rod that projected through the outer steel plating of the vessel close to the keel, the centerline at the bottom of a vessel's hull. The revolutions were recorded electrically on a clock in the chart room on the bridge.

Anything protruding through the bottom of a ship obviously increases its draft, the distance between the surface of the water and the lowest point of the vessel. Even though the Chernikeeff only increased draft by about one foot, it needed to be retracted when entering port. That meant pulling it up through the outer shell of the vessel and into a watertight gland for storage and safekeeping. As soon as the log was in position, a retaining screw was tightened, and another screw was secured to seal the log in place and make it waterproof from the inside. So to take the log in, two screws had to be loosened, one from the inside to allow the log to be pulled back up through the gland, and once in, another screw to dismantle the whole thing once the seacock, a valve on the hull that permitted water to flow into the vessel, was shut.

The Chernikeeff was positioned in the lowest part of the ship. To get there, you had to take the engine room elevator to the central engine control plate then pass through a watertight door to the double bottom tank hatch covers. The fourth officer gave Cadet Parry and me instructions on how to extract the Chernikeeff, so off we went. Opening the hatch covers revealed the upper handle of the log. As instructed, Mr. Parry went down into the tank while I remained above to shut the seacock. To do that meant bending down to turn the handle of the cock, which was above Parry's head.

At first, all went well as Parry undid the first screw with a two-headed wrench. I bent down and closed the seacock, which should have closed the aperture, which we both thought was now clear of all obstruction since we had pulled the log up as far as it would go.

That was not the case.

There was a pressure of water coming into the confined space where Parry crouched. I told him not to use the wrench again then bent down again and gave the seacock another hard twist, hoping that that would reduce the pressure. But the water pressure continued, and now I was really scared. Parry could not get out of the manhole while the brass log was sticking up through the hole. Our efforts to push it down were to no avail, and the water between the bilge keel and frame of the ship was deepening.

I braced my back against one wall of the compartment we were in and put both feet against the other. I grasped the head of the brass log and heaved with all my force. It slowly bent a few inches, thus widening the space for Parry to get out. I grasped Parry's raised hand, and he stood up slightly, but he would never make it through the small space that my efforts had made. Then the entire brass log shot out of the manhole. How it missed Parry, I'll never know. But the brass log blasting out of the manhole undoubtedly saved his life.

Once I got him clear, we ran to the engine room, shouting for help then followed three of the engine room crew running toward the considerable leaks the RDP had suddenly sprung. The combined efforts of three crewmen got the manhole cover down, and all available pumps were soon working on that portion of the double bottom compartment.

Cadet Parry and I went up and made our report to the fourth officer that the log was no longer protruding from the bottom of the ship.

We were harder put to give an explanation about what had happened, and the captain of the ship was soon appraised of the inexplicable event. The vessel anchored at Hamilton and a diver was summoned.

The various meetings between the fourth officer and us cadets and one between the captain, the chief engineer, and the fourth officer did exonerate Parry and me from any blame. The captain stated the fourth officer should have been overseeing the operation personally. Fortunately, our lack of popularity with the fourth officer was only temporary. The diver's findings were never told to us.

#

My second voyage aboard the *RDP* was equally eventful, but of a more personal nature. It was natural that during the first meal at sea, the cadets surveyed the young ladies in second class and vice versa. But there was little interaction at first because the voyage from Liverpool to Plymouth, then to La Rochelle in France, and finally Santander, Coruna, and Vigo in Spain resulted in cadets having hurried meals at varied times that did not conform to the passenger mealtimes. Also, many passengers took trips ashore while the vessel was in those ports.

After leaving Vigo, the shipboard routine became more regular because our next port, Hamilton in Bermuda, was about six days away. As the vessel proceeded on her southwesterly course, ice cream took the place of beef tea at 11 am and 3 pm and dancing on deck took the place of dancing in the second-class lounge after the evening meal was over.

About two nights after leaving Vigo, I was off watch with two other cadets. We were standing on the lifeboat deck chatting. Before long, the orchestra struck up a popular tune of the time, and the dance floor started to fill up. Two young ladies were standing by the rail with their parents. One of my companions announced he was going to ask the taller young lady to dance and suggested I do the same with her shorter companion. I did.

It was an unforgettable dance. That young lady was Joan, who would become my wife and the mother of my three children.

Of course, that night no mention was made of any serious commitments between us. That would happen some three weeks later on the vessel's voyage to Valparaiso, Chile. It turned out that I had the Great Depression to thank for meeting Joan. Her father, William P. Gamon, had joined the Santiago office of Duncan Fox & Co, a Liverpool trading company. He was laid off when the depression struck, and the family left Chile in 1930 and returned to London where William opened a consulting firm. Fortunately, in 1932, Duncan Fox rehired him for the Santiago office and it was on that return journey to Chile aboard the *RDP* that Joan and I met.

For the next seven years, we were to have sporadic meetings when the ship was in Valparaiso or Santiago and Joan could get leave from her office to go meet the vessel, or when I could get time off and dash to Santiago to see her for a few hours. How heart-wrenching were the farewells during those seven years! How we counted the days between the last of them and the next wonderful hello. How we lived for each other's letters. How we somehow knew but never took for granted that we would marry once war was declared in 1939. What gratitude we felt when our prayers were answered, and we were able to make our dearest dreams come true thanks to Joan's dear Ma and Pa, who arranged and paid for her passage back to England.

The rest of our lives together formed for me a string of souvenirs that I will try to express so that whoever reads these recollections will know how truly happy our days together were. Not everything that happened during those years was happy. However, I do know that despite the sadness and fear, I was always on the receiving end of Joan's love. I hope that when we meet again, she will tell me that she has felt the same about my love for her.

#

In 1935, I left the *RDP*, which would go on to become infamous in 1937 after former British Labour Prime Minister Ramsay MacDonald died aboard while on a cruise. During the Second World War, she was requisitioned as a troopship, serving with distinction in landings at North Africa, Sicily, and Normandy. In 1947, she was refurbished by her builder, Harland and Wolf, but soon after, a scavenge fire—caused by oil mist—and explosion killed 28 crewmen. In January 1948, the ship returned to her owners and was again refurbished for the Liverpool-Valparaiso service. After running aground in the Caribbean in 1957, she was scrapped in 1958.

RIP, *Reina del Pacifico*. Thanks to you, my whole life was given special meaning the moment I met Joan on your deck.

# Chapter Eight
# Prelude to War

I joined the King Edward VII Nautical School in London in January 1935 to sit for the Second Officer exam. The school was founded in 1902 by the British Sailors' Society to train Merchant Navy officers. It was located in the society's residential hostel for Marine Officers on London's West India Docks. (In 1969, it would move to a new location, and the building was turned into apartments in 1987.)

While I was studying there, my father rightly insisted that I draw unemployment. In England, it was known as *being on the dole*. The slang term was coined in 1919 by the *Daily Mail* newspaper, derived from the term *doling out*, which means handing out of charitable gifts of food or money. I felt my situation justified unemployment. The trouble, however, was that the office where I needed to pick up the money every Friday was in Chesham, a village about five miles from Chalfont where I was staying. There was no way to get there in time if I relied on the bus service. So my father lent me his car. I felt uncomfortable turning up in a car to stand in line for the dole. Most people perceived anyone on the dole as being down and out. So on one hand those in line might raise eyebrows about the car. On the other, my golfing friends might raise an eyebrow if they saw me in the line outside the Chesham dole office on any Friday morning.

To avoid recognition, I dressed in my oldest clothes, a raincoat—turning its collar up—and a hat I wore with the brim well down. Then I parked the car at a distance, which involved no connection with the labor office other than a long walk. But I couldn't stand the masquerade for more than a month. I obtained a transfer to Limehouse, the area of London where the school was located, for my Friday "banking." There I was among friends whose problems were similar to mine and far away from any golf course.

The examinations for the second officer, chief mate, and master are all similar in that the written portion deals with navigation, and the oral portion deals with seamanship and the use of instruments. Happily, I passed the written work without a problem, but I had grave misgivings about the oral part.

The examiners stressed the knowledge cadets had gained from their sea service. They were uniformly elderly men who had long since left active seagoing, and most were ex-tramp vessel masters, meaning they had served in vessels that traded in routes outside of those serviced by established shipping lines. A tramp vessel transports any cargo it can carry; therefore, they are never involved in passenger vessels. I had heard that the examiners had a preconceived opinion of cadets who had done their sea times in passenger vessels. Namely, that those cadets had spent most of their time dancing with passengers rather than learning all about the ship on which they were serving. This didn't bode well for me.

My fears were well-founded. After answering all the expected questions about correcting sextant errors and magnetic compass errors followed by an hour on questions about rules of the road with all kinds of vessel models, I felt that I had done well. Then we came to questions about the last ship I had served, and I had to say it was a large, modern passenger vessel. He wanted me to draw on a piece of paper the inside of the hydraulic, electric steering system as well as details of the davits, the crane-like devices used to lower the lifeboats. No way could I do that, and he expressed the opinion that anything I did not know about seamanship could only be learned at sea. The examiner gave me two months to go back there, learn it, and take the oral exam again.

I was really downcast because the questions asked did not involve the duties of a deck officer. I immediately received an appointment from PSNC to return to sea aboard the *MV Lautaro*, so away I went again but this time aboard the company's oldest ships which most certainly was not fitted with any modern devices. The most worrying aspect of the next few months was getting back in time to take and pass my oral exam before the validity of my written exam expired.

To cut a long story short, the school agreed to extend the validity of my written exam until after I retook the orals. My new examiner had the alarming name of Captain Kidd, but he announced that I had passed. Curiously, he asked me who my previous examiner had been.

My next appointment was as the fourth officer on the passenger vessel *SS Orbita*, a steamship headed by Captain Kirkwood. The chief officer was named Matthew

Armstrong, who made it a happy ship during the two years I was aboard. After that, it was exam time again, now for chief officer. That time, I had no problems with my orals, so in 1938, I was appointed the Second Officer of the *MV Losada*. After my first voyage, Matt Armstrong was appointed captain of that ship. It was good to be with him again.

Beginning in 1933, the name Adolph Hitler had sullied the press with ever-increasing frequency. I had taken little interest in British politics because the wars that had occurred in Spain and in the Gran Chaco between Bolivia and Paraguay seemed nearer geographically to my sphere of activities during that time. I was so glad and thankful that the world had climbed out of its economic pit, which had made the future for the youth of Britain look so depressing. While studying at the nautical college for the second officer certificate, I saw ex-students with master's certificates eating scant meals at the lunch counter and soliciting the young students' sisters and mothers to buy ladies' underwear.

At least the prospects were good now, and every day I awaited instructions for me to do my Royal Navy Reserve training. I knew enough about the world and its history in the making to expect those instructions very soon.

# Chapter Nine
# World War II

I never took special notice of what the British government of the day was doing while I was at sea in the pre-war days, maintaining ignorance of what transpired between the first and second world wars.

Much has been written about the Treaty of Versailles which was signed after World War I between the victorious Allies (United States, France, the UK, and others) on one side, and defeated Germany on the other. The Allies wrote the treaty with almost no participation by the Germans. The French wanted to dismember Germany to make it impossible for it to again wage war against France; the British and Americans did not want to exacerbate the tensions. The eventual treaty included 15 parts and 440 articles, which include many sanctions against Germany.

Part I created the new League of Nations, which Germany was not allowed to join until 1926. Part II detailed Germany's new boundaries, including giving Alsace-Lorraine back to France. Part III stipulated a demilitarized zone. Part IV stripped Germany of all its colonies. Part V reduced Germany's armed forces to very low levels and prohibited Germany from possessing certain classes of weapons. Part VIII called for reparations from Germany "as a consequence of the war imposed upon them by the aggression of Germany and her allies." Part IX imposed other financial obligations upon Germany.

The German government signed the treaty but under protest. Right-wing groups called the treaty a betrayal. Several politicians were assassinated. The US Senate refused to ratify the treaty. For five years, the French and the Belgians aggressively tried to enforce the treaty, which included a brief occupation of the Ruhr region of Germany. Britain and the US used economic pressure to convince France to end the occupation and agree to modify certain provisions of the treaty in an effort to promote German reparations. But Germany stopped paying during the Great Depression and violated many disarmament provisions of Part V. In 1935, Hitler denounced the treaty altogether, building up its aircraft and military equipment. When Hitler felt Nazi Germany was sufficiently strong to avenge the humiliations of World War I, his troops occupied Austria and Czechoslovakia in 1938. One can never know whether more rigorous enforcement of the original treaty or a more generous treaty would have avoided a new war. Perhaps a second World War was inevitable because of unresolved, lingering resentments.

Surely though, the least that each of the countries that contributed to Germany's defeat in WWI could do was make sure that Germany could not rearm. But nothing that they did after 1918 indicated that they were prepared to defeat Nazism when it reared its ugly head in 1932. In September 1938, Prime Minister Neville Chamberlain signed a peace pact with Hitler in Berlin. Knowing what we know now, the photos of Chamberlain waving the signed paper to the boisterous crowd at the airport upon his return from Germany are pitiful to view. Once confident that the UK would not interfere with his plans for Europe, Hitler occupied Poland on September 1, 1939, which started World War II.

At the time, the *Losada* was in the Colombian Pacific port of Buenaventura, still on our outward journey to Chile. I was grateful that the chances were good Joan and I would see each other again before my naval service was to start. Happily, she was able to come down to Valparaiso to meet the ship. Since our stay would be a short and busy one, the captain kindly invited Joan to spend the night aboard in one of the passenger cabins.

Before leaving port, the bridge was protected with sandbags to prepare us for the Atlantic crossing back to Liverpool. From Panama, we went straight up to Halifax in Nova Scotia where we joined the first convoy of the war. There were 60 ships in that convoy, and our escort was the cruiser *HMS Resolution*. The main danger at that time was Hitler's pocket battleships that might have had time to break out into the Atlantic, but the *Resolution* had the firepower to tackle one of them. It was believed submarines were not yet deployed in the Atlantic, so a torpedo attack was not considered likely. Fortunately, we arrived safely at Liverpool, where I received my orders to report to *HMS Drake* naval base at Devonport in Devon.

All officers in the Royal Naval Reserve, both in peacetime and wartime, were required to take the gunnery course at *HMS Drake*. I was one of about 30 midshipmen aspiring to become sub-lieutenants. The course lasted three weeks and comprised all aspects of naval gunnery control that existed in the latest battleships, cruisers, and destroyers. The course included drilling platoons of men for naval occasions, which reminded me so much of my officer training college days at Haileybury.

While I was at Devonport, I sent a cable to Joan's parents in Santiago, Chile, and asked for their help in arranging her passage to England. I was afraid that my action might appear presumptuous, but I knew they would appreciate my position now that England had declared war. Indeed they did. About ten days later, I received a message that Joan would soon be on her way.

What a happy day that was for me!

Since there was no air travel in those days, Joan would have to travel from Valparaiso to New York and from there to Liverpool by convoy. I did not know there was some difficulty with getting from Valparaiso to New York. The passenger vessels were not running as in peacetime and the berths for a single woman in a freighter were restricted to a minimum of two such passengers. Fortunately, the Ned Lloyd freighter *MV Sessa* was due to sail, and at the last minute, another female passenger also took passage to New York. It was a most fortunate break.

Once in New York, Joan had to wait there for the next fast convoy; she finally boarded the *RMS Samaria*, a week later. (Vessels having the right to carry mail for Royal Mail can use RMS—Royal Mail Service—as a prefix. Only contracted vessels have the right to use it.) Apparently, the manager of Duncan Fox in New York made her stay in New York very pleasant. Meanwhile, back at the gunnery course,

I knew nothing of Joan's movements but prayed that all would go well for her.

#

*January 6, 1940*
*HMS Drake:*

*Sweetheart, Joan*

*I was overjoyed to get your last two letters and to hear that you had had my wire—even more overjoyed to hear that you would be leaving soon. I am addressing this to New York because I feel certain that you have left before it can get to [Valparaiso].*

*Darling mine, I know just how you will feel at leaving the family behind and sailing off alone on a long voyage with all the uncertainties that life holds for us these days. You must know how much I would like to be with you and cheer you up, but I also know that you are very capable of facing anything that comes along and particularly of bearing those goodbyes. You always struck me as being a perfect heroine in that way. I can also imagine that your Ma and Pa will be feeling rather worried, and I can well understand that. I also feel worried, dearest, because on your voyage home I am powerless to do anything whereas when you are here, I can at least do my utmost to make you happy and comfortable.*

*I am going to write to your Ma and Pa and tell them as far as possible what I intend to do. Naturally, just as soon as is possible we shall be married, and that date of course depends on where I am at the time of your arrival in this country...*

*Please remember that Aveen [the family home] is open to you first as soon as you arrive, and I have been told to tell you that you will be most welcome either there or at my sister's place in Reigate. So if there is any danger of me not being able to meet you, you must phone or wire home and...you will be rescued by someone.*

*I finished my course here yesterday, officially. I did quite well in the examination in gunnery, which earned me six weeks seniority in the service, and now I am just wait [sic] to be appointed...*

*By the time you read this you will have completed the longest part of your journey and darling I do hope it has been pleasant... How I shall be longing to see you to hear all about everything. I shall write another letter to New York as soon as I hear where I am going to and when...*

*Hoping and praying for safety and happiness ever, ever yours only, Dick.*

#

We had little relaxation during our gunnery training, but there was always a reason for a little humor. The drill sergeant was a warrant officer while we, his students, were officers. This restricted him in the terminology he used whenever something did not meet with his approval. Once, he ordered two ranks of officers to face each other. Once our shuffling feet stopped, there was silence.

The drill sergeant announced in his usual loud voice: "We will now take our partners for the Lancers."

The Lancers is a well-known old English dance. When the general laugh had subsided, it took a little time before the platoon assumed some semblance of naval order.

# Chapter Ten
# Magnetic Mines

The course ended officially on December 31, but the new appointments were not expected for about a week. On the evening of January 6, I went to a movie in Plymouth with some colleagues. When we returned to the naval barracks, one of the guards at the gate called my name and handed me an envelope.

I opened it immediately and read my new appointment:

"Report aboard HMS Borde at 0700 hours January 8, 1940, at Sheerness, Kent, for duty as navigation officer."

After checking the trains, I called my father at home and asked him to meet the train at Paddington Station in London at about 5 pm the next evening, January 7, which he did. I asked him to take home some of my belongings such as a sword and dress uniform. Then I took a taxi to Liverpool Station for the train to Chatham Naval Base.

There were no bunks available at Chatham, so I was shown a mattress, pillow, and blanket in the billiard room where others were already asleep. I was told that a car would pick me up at 0600 hours and take me to Sheerness, at the mouth of the River Medway. That is where my war duty would begin.

Adolf Hitler had wasted no time after war was declared in warning the Allies that he had a secret weapon that would make his victory certain and quick. It soon became clear that the weapon was involved with the large number of vessels being sunk along the coasts of the British Isles. Hitler was convinced he could starve us into submission by cutting off our supplies even before his submarines had time to attack our convoys in the Atlantic Ocean. And in truth, the situation was critical by October 1939.

The secret weapon sinking our ships close to our ports had to be magnetic mines. Since the earth is in itself a very large magnet with its north pole in the Arctic and its south pole in the Antarctic, anything and anyone is exposed to the lines of magnetic force that join the two poles. But metal objects are the most easily magnetized. The softer the object's metal, the more easily it's magnetized. So steel, which is hard, is not as easily magnetized as iron.

Magnetized metal objects in the northern hemisphere have their North Poles in the end nearest the North Pole. In the Southern Hemisphere, the South Pole has a greater magnetic force resulting in a stronger south polarity for the end of the object nearest that pole. The intensity of a magnetic field is measured in gauss, named after Carl Friedrich Gauss, a German mathematician considered a pioneer of electromagnetism.

You can magnetize a metal object more quickly by tapping it with another metal object while it is within the lines of Earth's magnetic force between the two poles. So it's easy to see how great the magnetic field of a vessel can become during the building process. That magnetism has been reduced by shipyards building vessels positioned in an east/west direction, reducing the propensity of the metal to absorb the Earth's magnetism.

All this explains why a ship made of any metal is a floating magnet with a considerable magnetic field and a dominating north polarity if it was built in the Northern Hemisphere. Magnetism in a ship's structures has always been a problem because for many years we've had to rely on magnetic needles in our compasses to indicate which way the ship was moving.

In World War II, Hitler proved that a ship's magnetic field could be used to detonate explosive charges— magnetic mines—lying on the bottom of the sea. Because water is an incompressible element, it made the explosion more effective. Underwater explosions broke ship keels and breached submarine hulls. After the first mine detonated, the possibility of more mines discouraged sea traffic in the area, bringing merchant shipping to a standstill and draining manpower and materials for mine-spotting and (hopefully) disposal.

In truth, Hitler's secret weapon wasn't really a secret at all because Germany had simply exploited British magnetic mine technology from World War I to produce its own magnetic mine to use at the start of World War II. It was a technical surprise that cost the British dearly in the war's early months. And on January 8, 1940, magnetism was about to be a matter of life or death for me.

In simple terms, the magnetic mines laid by Germany in 1939 were containers holding a large explosive charge that was detonated by an electric circuit. The mines were laid either by submarine or by aircraft with parachutes. Once the container reached the seabed, an intricate device gradually brought the detonating circuit into a level position regardless of the position the mine had come to rest. Once that was done, a magnetic needle in the circuitry became exposed to any magnetic force outside the mine. (Magnetism is as effective in water as it is in the atmosphere.)

When the north end of that needle was exposed to the magnetic force from the north end of another magnet, it would repel it and close the circuit, thus detonating the mine. As already stated, the enormous water hammer created by the explosion on the seabed sinks the vessel immediately above it. The one limiting factor for using a magnetic mine was water depth. The deeper the water, the less the efficacy of the mine because of the distance between the mine and its intended victim.

The most important thing about magnetism and its forces is that when like poles meet, the magnets are repelled, and when unlike poles meet, the magnets are attracted. Bearing that in mind, we were certain that Hitler would be sure his mines were designed to sink vessels built in the northern hemisphere because there were so few vessels around that had been built in the southern hemisphere. The polarity of those few vessels built below the equator would allow them to pass over a mine without harm because their south polarity would attract it the needle in the mine, not repel it.

It was suspected that the first magnetic mines were laid by a submarine in the Thames estuary immediately after war was declared. By the end of September, the entrance to

London via the Thames estuary was blocked by mines clearly of the magnetic detonation type. Almost every large port in the British Isles could be closed to commercial traffic, so vital to the welfare of the population. By the end of October 1939, the sinking of commercial shipping around the coasts of the United Kingdom was definitely endangering the British war effort. During November and December, it was calculated that more than 200,000 tons of Allied and neutral shipping had been sunk around the British Isles by magnetic mines. It was clear that emergency measures were needed to keep British ports clear of German magnetic mines. Otherwise, Hitler's boast about his secret weapon might be justified.

In the early morning of November 22, 1939, as the ebb tide in the Thames estuary off Shoeburyness reached its low-tide level, a lookout reported an object on one of the mudflats. It turned out to be a magnetic mine that had obviously been released from a German aircraft during the previous night's air raid. It was an invaluable piece of luck, and no time was lost in examining the mine in detail. A naval officer named Lieutenant-Commander John Ouvry approached the mine with a set of non-magnetic tools, a portable telephone, and a lot of courage. Years later, he described the moment.

"We decided that Chief Petty Officer Baldwin and I should endeavor to remove the vital fittings; Lieutenant-Commander Lewis and Able Seaman Vearncombe to watch from what was considered to be a safe distance and make detailed notes of our actions and progress for reference in case of accidents. There was a possibility

67

that the mine had devices other than the magnetic one, which added to the hazard. If we were unlucky, the notes which the two watchers had taken would be available for those who would have to deal with the next available specimen.

"I first tackled an aluminum fitting sealed with tallow. In order to use one of the special [wrenches] which had been rushed through (by Commander Maton) in the local workshops for us, it was necessary to bend clear a small strip of copper. That done, we were able to extract this first fitting. Screwed into its base when we drew it clear, we found a small cylinder—obviously, a detonator, for in the recess from which the fitting had been withdrawn were disks of explosive. These I removed. This mysterious fitting proved to be a delay action bomb fuse; it was necessary for the airman to tear off the copper strip referred to (before releasing his load) if [a] bomb, not mine, was the requirement.

"Before we could proceed further, we had to call on Commander Lewis and Able Seaman Vearncombe for assistance to roll the mine over, this being firmly embedded in the hard sand and held fast by tubular horns. The fact that the mine did not and was not intended to float explains the non-success of our minesweepers in their efforts to secure a specimen. Lieutenant-Commander Lewis and Able Seaman Vearncombe from then onwards lent a hand with the stripping down.

"Dr. Wood, the chief scientist of the Mine Design Department, *HMS Vernon*, arrived in time to witness the later stages. We were somewhat startled to discover yet another detonator and priming charge. Having removed all the external fittings, we signaled for the caterpillar tractor and soon had the mine ashore. We had a shock—and a laugh when the shock wore off—before we had stowed away all the removed gadgets. We stopped for a breather on the foreshore, and one of the helpers carrying a rather heavy fitting put it down—on a stone. It immediately began to tick noisily. The company dispersed like lightning! That most disturbing ticking, we presently discovered, came from clockwork mechanism within the heavy fitting; actuated by pressure, it happened to rest on its starting spindle. This proved to be a delay-action device, designed to keep the mine safe until the clock setting had run off."

His task completed, the mine was removed to *HMS Vernon*, the Naval Mine and Torpedo Base at Portsmouth.

# Chapter Eleven
# HMS Borde

Taking events in chronological order after the examination of the mine was completed, the projected mine detector vessel operation went ahead. Since there was no time to build non-magnetic ships, the only other solution was to use a ship with a tremendous magnetic field that would detonate mines at a safe distance ahead of it. Such an emergency vessel could do wonders in keeping at least one of the channels leading to the port of London free of mines. So the Royal Navy commandeered the *HMS Borde*, an old, 2000-ton coast vessel, and fitted her hold with a 400-ton electromagnet—a type of magnet in which the magnetic field is produced by an electric current—that was about eight feet in diameter and supplied with considerable electric current from special generators. It was calculated that mines would be detonated about 50 yards ahead of the vessel.

The *HMS Borde's* engine room could accommodate the necessary electrical generators to produce over 2,000 MPs around the windings of the magnet our experts had calculated would produce a magnetic field of sufficient size and power to activate the magnetic needle detonator in any mine at least 150 feet ahead of the vessel.

The *HMS Borde* has been described in some reports as a mine detector vessel, or MDV. She has also been described as a magnetic minesweeper. There was—and to the best of my knowledge, still is—only one way to detect a magnetic mine and still be alive to report it. That is by detonating it intentionally. This was *Borde's* objective when the admiralty devised our operation on January 8, 1940. It was clear that our expedition was an act of desperation.

If successful in doing detection, then clearly she could become a sweeper too. So our success became of vital importance. We were either about to prove the efficacy of one system of detection as well as contributing to the war effort by keeping the approaches to London open for commercial shipping, or we'd become another victim of Hitler's weapon.

#

*January 8, 1940*
*HMS Borde:*

*Joan, sweetheart, darling mine,*

*Welcome home! Darling dearest do wish I could be in Liverpool to say this to you personally. You know that has always been one of my most precious dreams, but if it can't be so then I don't grumble. I only hope that you have had a pleasant voyage in every way. Sweetheart, I can't tell you where I am or anything about myself, but you understand why that is. As soon as possible...I shall get what leave I can.*

*I have asked a representative of the Cunard White Star to meet you on arrival and help you with customs etc. and about your movements from Liverpool. Kindly remember like a good girl, that the paying business for these services is arranged and you have nothing to do*

*So I think the best thing for you to do is to decide yourself where you would prefer to go first, and then tell Mum and Dad by telephone what you intend to do. I would love you to go home, so that I could meet you somewhere as soon as I get leave.*

*Being at sea makes things so difficult for me but I know, Joan darling, that you realize how difficult my position is. If you do stay with relatives and have a telephone number that you can leave, I'll phone you up at the first opportunity and will arrange a meeting. Of course if you go home, I'll dash there as soon as I get leave.*

*Our position is so difficult here. We are usually capable of getting leave of some sort every week or so but not for very long at a time. But as soon as I am ashore, and know where you are, I'll get into contact with you somehow, and will arrange something...*

*Again, welcome home to a troubled England. I'm afraid, but don't let that worry you. Ever, ever yours, sweetheart, Dick!*

#

As we started our operations on January 8, we were joined by a Vickers Wellington bomber fitted with a circular electromagnet over the wings and fuselage, which turned it into a mine detonator. I had the pleasure of meeting the aviator and was quite surprised when he told us that flying low over the water, about 25 feet up, was more dangerous than slow-motion exposure to an explosion under the vessel. We saw him detonate a mine, and it looked quite hairy when the plume of water arose behind his aircraft. He said he hardly felt it but had to get altitude as soon as possible. I realized an aircraft would never be a minesweeper because there were few means in the air of pinpointing one's position. On the water, you could lay small floating buoys with light anchors to mark the courses already steered by the vessel.

I had laid my charts out on a folding board fitted to the forward side of a shelter in the starboard wing of the bridge. That shelter had a glass front with a solid roof. The advantage of that position was that it looked out at the direction the vessel was steaming. I penciled in one set of arrows on the chart to indicate the direction of the tide at various times of the day and other arrows to suggest how our course might be affected by wind.

I had set the ship's course to pass right down the middle of the minefield and had presented it to Captain Hudson as soon as we left Sheerness. He had agreed to it, which is always comforting to a navigator who is not also the captain of a ship. My capabilities as a navigator would not be on display that morning. All I could do was to make vague calculations I knew were not accurate because the wind and tide were having a serious effect on the vessel. It was very comforting to know that a navigation specialist such as our captain would have no way of doing anything more under those circumstances.

While the *HMS Borde* was the first coastal commercial vessel to be fitted with the large 400-ton magnet, other vessels of the same type were planned, pending the results of our operation on that day. As we awaited the 7 am sailing time, Captain Hudson explained the air cushions we were standing on would protect our ankles whenever mine explosions occurred. He told us nobody was allowed forward of the bridge while we were sweeping. He pointed out two trawlers fitted with minesweeping equipment for any moored, or contact, mines we might encounter in our path to the magnetic minefield. He noted also the two wooden trawlers that would follow us closely in the minefield to lay the buoys, called dans, which would mark the center of the area we had swept on each course.

Captain Hudson didn't know what the small fishing vessel alongside us was doing and told the signalman to go down to the main deck and ask the skipper of that craft if he was with our party. Five minutes later, the signalman came back and reported with bated breath, "He has instructions to pick up any survivors."

On that happy note, we sailed down the River Medway toward the estuary of the Thames. About ten minutes before entering the minefield, the captain gave the order to activate the magnet. The secrecy of our raison d'être was soon highlighted when, on reaching the point at which the mined area began, we turned toward it. Our two sweepers ahead started to blow emergency siren signals—two short and one long—indicating danger.

I glanced at Captain Hudson, who assured me, "Take no notice. They don't know."

Now everything changed. I was ordered to put the vessel on our first course through the mined area marked on the chart. The main engine's revolutions slowed the vessel to six knots, and the unmistakable sound of the generators laboring indicated that the vessel had assumed the noble role of a magnetic mine detector. She would tell us in a very different way from that of the normal minesweeper that the enemy had been detected. She would detonate the mine 50 yards ahead of us, not astern as in known minesweeping. These thoughts went through my head along with the normal sensation of fear.

As we started our mine-detecting in earnest, it started to sleet, and visibility reduced accordingly. There we were heading into a known minefield. In all my navigation experience up to that point, my normal duties would have been to avoid that hazard like the plague. I was the navigator and would normally be responsible for the vessel's course, but we were steering in accordance with the captain's instructions, so the whole matter had been taken out of my hands.

There was no conversation. Everyone was under the strain of knowing that at any moment we might get blown out of the water. Captain Hudson was standing bolt upright looking forward. The helmsman was steering the vessel and keeping it on course, and the lookouts were on each side of the bridge peering in the direction the vessel was moving. I glanced at the compass repeater every now and then to make sure we were on course and constantly checked to make sure that the trawler was laying buoys every 50 yards or so.

I have tried to remember what I was thinking about as we approached our first mine. I know that my main thoughts were of Joan who was on her way to England to marry me. I was hoping that she was safe in every way and that I would survive the day and be there when she arrived. I knew, however, that thinking of her at that moment was not appropriate.

Because we were standing over the south end of the largest electromagnet the world had known at that time, the *Borde* was not fitted with a magnetic compass. Instead, we had a gyrocompass, which worked on the principle that a spinning object always maintains its axis at right angles to the axis of the earth. However, I noticed that the specialists had placed corrector magnets around the gyro to counteract the effects of the enormous magnetic field it was creating.

I became very much aware of how inexact our course could be if the effects of tide and wind were not accurate. Then I realized there was no one on board who was remotely interested if we were a mile out when we reached the far side of the minefield.

There was a shudder, and the old ship appeared to sit up and beg for an instant as the highest, thickest column of water I had ever seen shot up in front of us. Then half of it fell on the ship. But all we cared about was that we got the mine and not vice versa. When the water cleared, we could see the woodwork along the front of the bridge was shaken out of the true and was leaning outward. All the glasswork had broken, but the roof over the cab where my chart was had done a good job protecting it.

Before we had time to complete our damage survey, there was another explosion. On its way down, the water this time took advantage of the holes in the bridge structure created the first one and wet a bit more of my chart but never mind that. I laid the position of the exploded mines on the chart and drew a line between them. They still ran along the deep-water channel a submarine would proceed up. About 20 minutes later, we arrived at the farthest end of the minefield, and Captain Hudson turned the vessel to return on a reciprocal course. I showed him where I had plotted the first two mines and boldly suggested they might be two of a line of mines we should be reaching at six minutes past the hour by my watch. I watched the moments tick away.

*Bang!*

But this time something was different. Eerily different. The whistle from the engine room voice pipe sounded almost simultaneously followed by hurried steps coming up the ladder to the bridge.

The chief engineer breathlessly stated, "We have lost the power on the magnet, sir."

Captain Hudson immediately ordered, "Full speed astern." The old girl started to shudder as the engine was reversed. He came to the wing of the bridge and peered over the side, and when he saw that the ship was no longer moving ahead, Captain Hudson ordered: "Stop the engine."

So we lay there, the only sounds were the icy breeze through our rigging and the muted conversation between the captain and the chief engineer about the possible cause for this loss of power. Only seconds passed before the engineer was heading back to his domain with the captain's instructions to "let me know when you are ready to put the power on again."

I think that I can best describe the next few minutes as a white-knuckle moment par excellence because we were without a doubt in the middle of a known minefield. If repair of the problem were to take a considerable time, we would have to get out of the minefield by the shortest route because we were the most magnetic vessel in the world, and any mines around might be a lot less than 50 yards away. If the reason for the loss of power was evident and easily repaired, and if we put the power on again, would we blow ourselves up if a mine was within 30 yards or less? Either way, Captain Hudson would have to give an order without any idea what the result would be.

When the chief engineer announced through the voice pipe that he was now ready to power up, Captain Hudson could only say, "Put the power on the magnet."

The exhaust of the large generator was very audible. As soon as the sound of idling turned to a laboring throb, the captain gave the order, "Engine slow ahead."

A count of ten later, there was another explosion and the now-familiar enormous column of seawater rising in front of us was followed by an even greater surge of relief and gratitude for having survived. The unmistakable flutter of wings was proof once more of my guardian angel's presence.

It was getting dark, so we proceeded out of the minefield to find a safe anchorage. But it appeared that the windlass, the machinery used for hoisting the anchor in, was lying in several pieces on the forecastle—the raised deck at the bow of the ship—so if we ever anchored, there would be no way of weighing it again.

Captain Hudson arranged to have one of the larger minesweeping trawlers that were still waiting for us outside the minefield drop both its anchors so we could tie up the *Borde* alongside it until daylight when we would have to return to Chatham. But the trawler's anchors were not heavy enough to hold both vessels in the strong tidal current, so in order not to endanger both vessels, our captain decided to cast off and do what we could on our own not to run aground on the Goodwin Sands—a ten-mile long sandbank—or hit one of the many wrecks in the area which were marked with buoys without lights.

So started a hit-and-miss night; we hoped there would be no hits and that we would miss all the dangers; we had no means to avoid since we could not fix our position. None of the city lights of Dover and Folkestone, which in peacetime would be casting their reflections against the low clouds, nor any of our navigation lights were lit as a precautionary measure against submarine minelayers, enemy surface vessels, and air-raids.

As the navigator, I felt responsible to do something to avoid running aground, which strangely enough seemed the only danger that night. We received a radio message that after we had left the minefield, the *SS Simon Bolivar*, a Dutch passenger vessel on its way to South America, was sunk by a German magnetic mine. Sadly, there was much loss of life.

That affected Captain Hudson a lot. He told me afterward that he felt responsible for having to call off our minesweeping operations so soon that day, even though the mine that sunk the *Simon Bolivar* was actually not near the minefield where we were operating.

While we were drifting around in the Goodwin Sands area that night, magnetic mines did not seem too great a menace because the channels leading into the Thames estuary from the south had been considered clear of mines. Languishing on a sandbank, with our vessel a total loss, seemed to be the number one danger. Being holed by hitting the sunken carcass of a wrecked vessel on a sandbank seemed to be danger number two. We took turns sleeping that night. Captain Hudson slept in the chart house on the bridge for about three hours while I and another officer, Lt. Morris, each took the three hours watches between 8 pm and 2 am. It was just about 11 pm when the *Borde* shuddered ever so slightly, and the portside lookout shone his flashlight over the side and shouted to me.

I dashed over and saw a large, round buoy marked: *Wreck*. The buoy was still bearing signs of green paint. I dashed to the chart and for the first time since it got dark was able to tell the captain where we were.

He said, "See if you can stay with it."

The buoy was still there when I peered over the side again, but I could see from the water movement that we would soon be swept away from it by the strong tide. Happily, we hit no wreck, but the position of the buoy and the direction of the tide made it impossible for us to use our engines to stay there, particularly as the tide direction would be changing within the following two hours. I left the bridge an hour or so later, and my guardian angel took over until daylight. When I was awakened, we were entering the River Medway on our way to the Naval Base at Chatham.

It seems that the director of minesweeping at Bath, in Somerset, was satisfied that the operations during the first day of mine detection had been a success in that there were no casualties among the crew. However, the vessel had suffered enough damage to necessitate extending her magnetic field if she was to continue operating. The hull near the bow had been damaged as had the machinery on the forecastle. The damage to the bridge structure was easily repaired, but further damage at that distance from the bow was to be expected while mines were being detonated so close to the vessel.

Finding a way to extend the magnetic field was studied with great care because there was no way it could be increased using the 400-ton electromagnet. The only solution was to fit an additional magnet on the forecastle of the vessel, slightly inclined with its forward end higher. Additional power to feed the additional magnet was available from the generator we already had. Work was soon started on this alteration, and I was told it would take a month to make us operational again.

After our return to Chatham on January 9, I called home and was given the good news that Joan had reached New York safely and was staying with friends there until the *Samaria* sailed for Liverpool—whenever that would be. That news had come from Joan's relatives in Chester where she was to stay until she received news from me.

No account of my life at this juncture could be complete without a few words about my feelings. The war was now about four months old. I had prayed and been granted my dearest wishes: that Joan would come to England and that she would reach the end of her journey safely. Naturally, she realized her journey would not be without danger. When I asked her to meet me in England, I didn't know what was in store for me because I was then still in gunnery training. Since then, things had changed. When we were last together in Valparaiso, we had talked about my naval service and married life in wartime. We had both mutually expressed that no life for either of us would be worthwhile unless we were married and living together, even under wartime conditions. Those words of mine now came back to haunt me. Why had I so glibly expressed myself when there was the very great probability that Joan would be on her way to marry me in England, and a good possibility that I might not be alive to greet her? I wondered if Joan now had the same qualms, but knowing her, I felt sure she may have never given this a thought. But then, why should she? She was not to know that I would be on board the first experimental magnetic minesweeper.

I had to tell somebody about my lack of thought for her wellbeing. She had to know that I was worried about her happiness should the worst happen to me. I had to tell somebody that I was sorry for having dragged her into a war from the happy family life she was enjoying. So I told my mother and father, and they assured me they would pass my message on to Joan if the need arose.

#

Shortly after resuming our mine-detonating operations, we were ordered to the northernmost channel in the Thames estuary that leads to and from the port of London. This meant we would make our base for provisions at Harwich and anchor closer to our operation area. Each morning, we received our milk, bread, fresh provisions, and the *Daily*

*Mail* newspaper, which the steward religiously laid on Captain Hudson's breakfast table. I noticed that he turned to the comics page first to read *Buck Ryan*, an adventure comic strip created by Jack Monk and writer Don Freeman.

Ryan was a young British private investigator who fights crime. His adversaries included a female crime boss named Twilight along with various kidnappers and German spies. The captain explained that he (superstitiously) tied Buck's daily activities to ours on the *Borde*. If things went well for Buck in that day's strip, it would go well with us.

That childish part of Captain Hudson's character intrigued me; it was unusual to find it in a 35-year-old naval officer who showed such intelligence in his daily activities searching for magnetic mines. One morning after reading about Buck, he brought up mines set to explode when approached by a vessel built in the southern hemisphere. I wasn't sure whether he had received something in the mail from the director of minesweeping (DMS) or whether it was just something that was on his mind, but clearly, he wanted to talk about it.

He went on to explain that any mine could be set to explode when either end of the compass needle in the detonator closed the electric circuit necessary for detonation. A mine set by Germans to sink ships built in the southern hemisphere would not sink many ships, but it would sink the *Borde* because the south pole of our magnet was right under our breakfast table. DMS had estimated that the German magnetic mine was an unnecessarily expensive item when compared with the one Britain had designed but never used at the end of World War I. Surely they would not lay a mine capable of sinking only one particular ship.

That thought remained in our minds during the months we exploded mines.

The winter of 1940 dragged on into April. Much of our sweeping was done in snow and sleet. We were reported sunk on several occasions during detonations by other ships miles away reporting explosions near a vessel which then disappeared. Many ships also reported that their compasses were being affected by some disturbance nearby.

One night in early May 1940, there was a heavy air raid on east coast British ports, mainly in the Tyne and Tees. The next night, we were told to proceed north to the Port of Blyth to detonate mines that had possibly been laid there. We left the Harwich area at about 8 pm, and I laid courses to Blyth up the channel swept for contact mines. When I came on watch again at midnight, I was surprised to see that Captain Hudson had ordered a change of course, and we were headed south. He left a cryptic note saying that DMS had ordered us back to Chatham.

I never knew the official reason for that sudden change of orders, and the captain appeared not to know either. Did it have anything to do with a south polarity mine laid 24 hours earlier in the Tees raid? Before long, I was convinced that it did. During those references to the possibility that the Germans might lay a rogue mine every now and then, Captain Hudson had said that there was a simple way for a mine destructor vessel to protect herself, but he wasn't sure the high cost involved would be justified. When I asked him to explain what the simple way was, he said that we would have to sweep with alternating current.

I had to admit that I did not understand how that would cover us against the north polarity mines we were having such success with.

"Oh no," he replied, "we would have to sweep with both. Say DC for six seconds then AC for six seconds."

On arrival at Chatham, Captain Hudson received a message that the ship was to be fitted with special breakers that would change the current supplied to the magnet from AC to DC every six seconds. All I could do was to thank my guardian angel once more and express a profound hope that the system would work. It must have done because we detonated three mines after fitting those breakers. But not even the captain could say whether they were south or north polarity mines, and now there was no point in knowing even though I know who knew.

The arrival of spring and summer saw much change in combating magnetic mines. By June 1940, there were two other magnetic mine detector ships in addition to the *Borde*, but they could never sweep a minefield clear of mines because the area they could cover was so narrow—about 30 x 100 yards. And obviously, they could never widen that path by sweeping together without grave risk. Clearly, the emergency measure of detonating magnetic mines ahead of the sweeper had to be changed, and the only way to do that was by demagnetizing the sweeper and then creating the field astern of it.

Wooden trawlers were first employed for that. They were fitted with generators supplying current to two buoyant lines, each with electrodes at the end that emitted 5-second pulses at 15-minute intervals. Two of these trawlers could operate side by side, the cables towed behind them, one with positive bursts and the other with negative bursts. The area covered by each pulse between the two trawlers was about ten acres or approximately 220 x 220 yards. It was called the *double L sweep*, and it put the finishing touch to Hitler's much-vaunted first secret weapon.

Mention has to be made here about the flexibility of the danger the German magnetic mine involved. Since detonation was created by closing an electric circuit, it was relatively easy to devise a system whereby a needle can be activated by a vessel without closing a circuit, thereby not detonating the mine. Mines with any number of such false needle deflections could be laid giving continuous indications to a sweeper that there were no mines in that area. Finally, a circuit is closed, and the Russian roulette finds a loser. I should also mention the sound mine, which is detonated by the noise of either a vessel's propeller or its engines.

During our various visits to the repair yard at Chatham, Captain Hudson studied the minesweeping that might have to be involved with those weapons. One morning, he came down to breakfast smiling and told us that he had done an Archimedes, as he called it. The *HMS Borde* was probably one of the few ships in the Royal Navy not fitted with showers. Being British-built and in an era when showers were unknown in the British Isles, getting clean was done by bathing, not showering as it is today. Captain Hudson noted that heating bath water was achieved by turning on a valve that blew live steam into the tub of cold water. When the steam was turned on, the cold water in the bath made a loud crackling sound. As the water in the bath heated, the sound disappeared.

In *HMS Borde,* we had plenty of steam and a commanding officer with time on his hands to devise schemes made necessary by war. The windlass used to raise the anchor was steam-operated, so with the help of the engine room staff, it was relatively easy to run a steam line from it to the water alongside the vessel. When the result was sufficiently satisfactory to warrant the spending of more time and energy on the project, Captain Hudson devised a diaphragm through which the crackling sound could be increased.

He and I spent hours walking around the wharves with metal tubes. We'd place one end in the dock water and the other to our ears while the engineer aboard made sure that the steam supply remained constant.

Germany had experimented with both the sound mine and the pressure mine, but neither I nor the captain was on the *Borde* when their detonation was involved by the Royal Navy. As the double L sweep was further developed, degaussing of all vessels became essential. The latter was done by running electric cables with the opposite polarity— so south polarity in the case of vessels built in the northern hemisphere—around the vessel at the main deck level. As soon as these cables were fitted, the vessels were run over degaussing meters to fingerprint the gauss readings to a level considered to be safe from magnetic mines. The degaussing meters were installed at the major ports, and special teams ensured that every vessel was considered safe before it was allowed to sea.

With the advancing technology, the *HMS Borde's* part in minesweeping became redundant. Where the *Borde* was concerned, the reduction of gauss readings had to present difficulties. Our magnet was poison, so in September 1940, we proceeded to dry dock at Blackwall in London and started the prolonged work of reducing our gauss count.

# Chapter Twelve
# The Blitzkrieg

Joan and I had gotten married in February 1940. After our honeymoon, Joan moved in with my parents at Chalfont while I was at sea. Whenever I had any time off, I went there. We often had to spend the night on mattresses in the hallway because of air raids. My father had joined the Home Guard, and every so often he had night duty.

The month of May 1940 was a sad one for the Allies. France fell to the German blitzkrieg and the British Army retreated from Dunkirk and back to England. The captain told me that I would have to stay with the vessel because I was the junior officer. He and Lt. Morris had to man small craft to help rescue soldiers at Dunkirk. Thankfully, they both came back. Now that it seemed probable that our stay at Blackwall might be longer than expected, we decided to look for rooms in London so I could be with Joan on my days off duty.

Another officer had joined *Borde* by this time. He was Sub-Lieutenant Rogers, a member of the Royal Navy Volunteer Reserve (RNVR). He was a very nice young man. Captain Hudson arranged for each of us to have 24 hours off duty every three days. So Joan and I were able to find a nice apartment in Kensington—with a bedroom, a sitting room with a kitchenette, and bathroom—and started the very first housekeeping experience of our married lives.

I am sorry to say that the very first pieces of furniture we supplied ourselves with were two ashtrays since we both smoked at that time. They were light-blue glass trays. I still keep them out as one of the very few ornaments here in Naples, a souvenir of those days 61 years ago.

The day that the *HMS Borde* entered dry dock at Blackwall started a new period of my life that was very different. The ship's company, from the captain down, now joined hands with the population of London to withstand the continuous dangers from nightly air raids. It was October 1940, a month when Hitler must have told Herman Goering that it was high time the Luftwaffe put an end to British resistance with bombs, both high explosive and incendiary ones. History has shown that the real Battle of Britain between the Royal Air Force (RAF) and the Luftwaffe was not being won by German air superiority.

Being aboard a ship in dry dock during an air raid was akin to an injured person being operated on atop the roof of an ammunition factory. It certainly would not need a direct hit to complete the damage. Captain Hudson had given me strict instructions that a gun crew should always be aboard so that our 12-pounder anti-aircraft gun could be manned should enemy aircraft be sighted. I never imagined that we would be ordered to fire it, but it was all we could do, and it was good for morale. To our relief, no enemy aircraft dared to come into sight.

I was very happy that Joan was somewhere near, so I could see her on my days off. But here again, I had grave doubts about securing accommodations for her in greater London, which was much more likely to be targeted by the enemy than Chalfont, where my parents lived. However, we talked about it, and Joan insisted that she would much sooner become a target if the enemy was that short of targets!

Despite her bravery, I still relived the fears that had assailed me a year earlier when Joan was on her way to England. Now that she was in London, we had to forego safety to be together during my days off. The Blitzkrieg had started on September 7 in 1940 with 300 German bombers raiding London. It was the first of 57 consecutive nights of bombing. After that, periodic bombing would continue until May 1941. The German air-raids were Teutonic in their regularity, and to me, that was something of a mystery. One would imagine that maintaining a strict schedule would help the RAF to be prepared but supposedly such schedules can be changed at short notice with grave results to the defenders.

I found that by purchasing a bicycle, I could reduce travel time between Kensington and Blackwall. Not because of velocity but because large traffic jams, bomb craters, and detours through side streets could be circumvented on a two-wheeled vehicle.

I fixed my route by keeping to the Commercial Road as far as Aldgate East tube station. From there, my direct route was through Leadenhall Street to the bank, past St Paul's Cathedral, up Ludgate Hill to the Aldwych Theater, then along the Strand, through the Admiralty Arch to Buckingham Palace, up Constitution Hill to the Victory Arch, then down Kensington High Street to Cromwell

Road. As I turned that corner, my heart was always in my mouth. Would our block of flats still be standing after the air raids the previous night?

London's air raid damage was a no-no for the media. As far as the news was concerned, none had been dropped unless someone had actually seen it. Word of mouth was the only way to find out where a bomb had landed or if you knew someone who had suffered the loss of life in their family. I always found it difficult not to panic until I could see with my own eyes that the building where we had our flat was still standing.

Much has been written about the aerial attacks on cities in the British Isles. Much has been written about the bravery of citizens of those cities. I am convinced that the extent of that bravery can never be known by anyone who was not among them during those nights and days of destruction and death. There were many deaths during each night of horror. And on each day that dawned, both soldiers and civilians knew full well that by the next dawning, there would be many more. What it takes to bear that suffering is surely a divine gift.

Onboard our ship, high and dry in a dock in the east end of London, we had gangs of workmen involved in the urgent work of getting the ship safe for her future operations of minesweeping. I will never forget the foreman. He was a very cheerful character and full of the sort of patriotism that maintained a happy gang of workers.

I was surprised one morning when the gang arrived on board without him. When I asked the assistant about that, I was told that he had heard that the foreman's house had suffered a near miss on the previous evening. The foreman appeared aboard about 10:30 am and told me he had been arranging funerals for two members of his family who had been killed the night before. I had a strong urge to say something to console him in what must surely have been deep grief but was stuttering for the appropriate words.

Then the look he gave me and the grip on my arm as he said, "Thanks, sir. I hope the work is going well," took the place of anything that I could have said and done to help him.

Memories of that man stayed with me for years, especially when I was particularly worried about the welfare of my own family and/or myself. How many thousands of other families must have suffered and faced that ordeal so bravely, only God knew.

Not long after that incident, Joan and I were to face what seemed like a direct attempt by the enemy to end our lives. One Sunday evening, we decided to see a movie. After a late lunch, we went to a theater near Piccadilly Circus. It was over around 6 pm and we came out into the dusk. As we got on a bus, the air raid sirens announced the arrival of enemy planes. Since we had a long ride to Fenchurch Street Station where we would take the train to Tilbury where Joan was staying, we decided against going to a shelter and stayed on the bus. There were three or four other passengers still on the bus as we went down Fleet Street to Ludgate Circus.

A light rain had started to fall. I recall so vividly the sight of incendiary bombs hitting the parapet surrounding the dome of St Paul's Cathedral, dancing in the steam they created as they hit surfaces.

A few moments later, the driver of the bus announced he would go no further because there were buildings alight in distant Fenchurch Street, which was our destination. We were the last two off the bus, and as we stepped to the sidewalk, we were greeted by a shower of the white-hot incendiaries. I do not know what would have become of us had we not seen a sheltered doorway a few yards away.

The bus had pulled away and disappeared into the smoke, which seemed to shroud the whole of London's business area, known as The City. Up until then, we had heard no explosions of falling bombs, but the incendiaries with their whirring sound and intense heat still rained down. We grabbed each other tightly in that doorway, which undoubtedly saved our lives.

We must have been there about ten minutes when a voice shouted to us from across the narrow street, and a flashlight shone in our direction. The man identified himself as an air raid warden and beckoned us to where he stood in the doorway of a shelter. We decided to risk it, and together we must have broken some kind of sprint record as we aimed ourselves at the flashlight and to the door of the shelter.

We went down a flight of stairs into a large cellar space where there were some 50 or 60 people sitting and laying— all drinking tea. Before long, we were doing likewise. Since I was in uniform, my actions were not as restricted as those of civilians. It was clearly for that reason that the air raid warden gave me a running report on how the air raid was progressing. One of his duties was to make routine visits to the roof of the building. We had been there about an hour when the warden asked me if I would like to see the sight from the roof, which I suppose must have been about five or six stories high. With Joan's permission, I made that fleeting visit, and what I saw was astounding. That particular night apparently marked the occasion when the German Luftwaffe's defeat started.

Thanks to the RAF, the daytime raids had been costly operations for the Germans in terms of planes and pilots. Consequently, on that Sunday evening, Hitler planned a final blow that would end all civilian resistance in London by setting it alight. Once that was achieved, the bombers would have no difficulty finding their targets.

*Get there, drop your bombs, and get out before the Spitfires see you* seemed to have been their orders. From my place on the roof of an office building on Leadenhall Street, I could see how devastating the incendiary raid had been. However, I could see nothing in the sky but thick clouds, which meant that the bombers had that exact same view from the other side. Providence had provided a thick cloud layer to protect our city. When the air raid was over at about 3 am, Joan and I were able to pick our way through the mass of water hoses and firemen dealing with the fires and finally get a train that got us to the Tilbury Hotel just as daylight was breaking. In the quiet of that hotel, I could hear the fluttering of those ever-present wings of my guardian angel, once again affording us protection.

#

The arrival of 1941 was to bring many changes for those of us on the *HMS Borde*. She bowed out of her role as an experimental detonator of magnetic mines and was now asked to play a smaller part in the campaign against magnetic mines for which she had to learn a very different script. She had to forget everything about using her magnetic power to detonate mines and learn just the opposite. I guess the naval authorities involved never heard that it's not easy to teach an old dog new tricks.

To assume her new role, electrical specialists joined our staff. I was promoted to executive officer (First Lieutenant) and received an honorable mention in dispatches. Sadly, my captain received another appointment in February after receiving the Distinguished Service Order. He joined the Commander in Chief of the Far East Fleet's staff as navigator aboard the *HMS Exeter*.

I am sure that I do not have to explain how friendships of a special kind can be forged in wartime when there is a common enemy, a common endeavor, and a common danger. Just as the captain of the *HMS Borde*, Roland Keith Hudson deserves a place in my narrative. But since I asked that my first male grandchild be given one of his names, I feel bound to say something more about him.

While he was very honest, he was a proponent of everything good. Aren't we all? Yes, but RKH was convinced that the word was first and foremost applicable to the Royal Navy. That made him a great naval officer despite the fact that he was self-effacing and shy. Having those adjectives applicable to a man with a very clever brain made him an excellent officer. I am sure that if he had not been, he would never have been chosen to command an experimental vessel such as the *Borde*. He had no hobbies other than the Royal Navy and playing the piano. The first he lived with; the latter he was not particularly good at, but that did not deter him from buying an upright and installing it in his office on board after the old ship was taken off active mine detonating. He could be heard tinkling away whenever there was nothing else that had to be done.

We had long conversations about everything because he was a mine of information and a very good listener. Though he was senior to me in rank, he appreciated that there was little difference in our ages. After the *HMS Exeter* sank during the Malacca Straits battle, he was taken prisoner by the Japanese and survived the ordeal. RKH was a deeply religious man, so I was not surprised to hear that as soon as the war ended, he left the navy and took Holy Orders. I have tried to contact any family that might be living in his hometown area of Bournemouth but without success.

#

I remained on the *Borde* four more months after RKH's reassignment. During that time, I have to say life was somewhat of an anti-climax. I believe we had all suffered from a certain amount of tension from the proximity of the mine detonations. I know that I now had an immediate and ill-tempered reaction to sudden noises, but it was nothing serious.

My new appointment was with the *HMS Whitehaven*, a new minesweeper being built in Dartmouth by George Philip & Son. There could not have been a better treatment for frayed nerves.

# Chapter Thirteen
## Foreign Service, 1942–1943

Back on the home front, it was clear that Kensington and Tilbury would not be appropriate places for Joan to call home much longer. In February 1941, Joan gave me the good news that she was expecting, and we decided to find a safer place for her to live. She also badly wanted to get a job; therefore, we needed a suitable place she could commute from and where I could visit her whenever my naval commitments permitted.

She applied for a job as secretary to the senior officer of the Air Force's coastal command, telling them upfront she would only be able to work for about six months. No matter. She was accepted, thanks largely to the many years she had worked in the British Embassy in Santiago, Chile. Her boss was a most accommodating man and asked her to just give him six weeks notice when she wanted to leave.

Getting the job made it clear that Northwood would have to be her next home. On one Saturday afternoon when I was on leave, we answered an ad in the paper for a flat in Northwood. The prospective landlord was at work, so we waited until the owner, Vernon, finally appeared to show us the flat. It was a great place but way beyond our means, which we made clear to him.

As we prepared to leave, he asked if we would accept a drink since we had waited so long, and it was Saturday after all. We accepted, and he poured us and himself a whiskey. The conversation turned to where we were from. When Joan said Chile, he said that the only thing he knew about that country was told to him by a relative who had been there for many years. Joan asked the relative's name.

Vernon said, "William Gamon."

Joan's father! Our host turned out to be a cousin Joan had heard her aunt in Chester talk about. We still did not get the flat, but Vernon certainly offered us another drink.

We did finally find a single bedroom flat that suited us very well and was within walking distance of Joan's work at the coastal command. So started 1941. In June, I received my appointment to the *HMS Whitehaven*, and it was then that Joan went to live with my mother and father in Chalfont. While there, I applied to get her a bed at Fulmer Chase, a maternity home for the wives of military officers that was the brainchild of Mrs. Winston Churchill, the prime minister's wife. It was close to Chalfont and offered full prenatal and postnatal services.

#

I arrived at Dartmouth to join the *HMS Whitehaven*, a Bangor class moored-mine fleet sweeper. Able to sweep for magnetic and acoustic mines, it was a class of vessel designed to operate in close conjunction with naval units supporting the army. She was just the opposite of the *Borde* in many ways. She was brand new, much faster, and swept mines by cutting their mooring lines with wires towing cutters, kites, and floats from the stem, the most forward part of a ship's bow. The kites in minesweeping are made of metal and use the water to do their job, which is to keep the cutters outside the course steered by the ship.

It seemed that for the rest of the war, I should expect to be sweeping mines. Though the procedure for doing that in the *Whitehaven* was new to me, I had plenty of time to become acquainted with it. George Philips & Son's shipyard was close to Dartmouth which made commuting very easy. When I reported to the naval officer in charge at Dartmouth, I was delighted to learn that I would be able to use the college as my pied-à-terre. So I finally made it!

The happy aspects of this period of my naval career were that I could travel to Chalfont to see Joan at weekends if I could afford it and the interesting people I met in this normally sleepy little town. Dartmouth was the base for a fleet of fast motor torpedo boats, which were commanded by young lieutenants who were great company during leisure hours in the evenings but very close-mouthed about their frequent expeditions. While there, I had the pleasure of meeting Lieutenant Sone, the naval officer in charge of the nearby fishing village, Brixham. The most interesting thing about him was that he was said to speak 14 languages and dialects. What was one man doing to learn that many? And what was he doing in Brixham?

I never found out the answer to the first question. Some weeks later I heard he was in the Secret Service, meaning he was a spy. That information was shared after I learned Lt. Sone failed to return from a Secret Service mission to

Italy. I wish I could have met Mrs. Sone and their children to express my condolences.

While I was at Dartmouth, I made a friendship so unforgettable that any account of my life would be incomplete without it. One afternoon, I was walking in an area of the town unknown to me. It was a Saturday afternoon, and as I passed a garage, I noticed a young long-haired German shepherd lying just inside the doorway. As I passed, he stood up, and I noticed he was chained.

I stopped as I always do to greet dogs that appear amenable and held out my hand at a safe distance. Since that caused no reason for complaint, I patted his head and received a tail-wag. Inside the door were two men working on a car. They stopped their work as I made a complimentary remark about the dog. This started a conversation, and one of the men explained how the dog was a refugee from an air raid on Plymouth a week earlier that had badly damaged the man's house. The other man was his brother-in-law who had given refuge to his sister's family and their dog. I offered to take the dog for a walk since I needed company and my offer was immediately accepted.

What faith the public has in a uniform!

To cut a long but very happy story short, I became the owner of Kym, or more correctly Kym of Kentwood. It was not surprising that Kym's arrival made it necessary for me to make certain changes in my lifestyle. Such as, I had to leave the college and find local digs where the landlord would accept my friend, Kym. Reference to the local newspapers led me to a lady who was willing to accept Kym and me for a reasonable bed and breakfast rate. Later, when the time was near for Clive to arrive and for the *Whitehaven* to be commissioned, I took Kym to meet Joan. At least she saw him that once out of the nursing room window before the sad day came when Kym and I had to part.

#

*My father's encounter with Kym, a long coat German shepherd and the camaraderie that developed during those times of great uncertainty, tells me of his tremendous love for animals, especially dogs and horses, which continued throughout his life. The same passion has been passed on. Thanks, Father; we shared the joy and sadness with so many beloved animals.*

*— Sylvia*

#

*November 2, 1941*
*Dartmouth, Devonshire, England*

*My darlingest Juanita.*

*I was delighted to get your letter on Saturday morning with the latest budget about yourself and Clive. I am so glad that Mum and Katze were able to see him and thought he was a nice baby.*

*Well, the new captain arrived yesterday afternoon, and I went down to meet him before dinner yesterday. He seems a charming chap as far as one can tell at present Next week and the week after are going to be pretty hectic as far as I can see. There seems to be plenty to be done, but I suppose we shall manage it somehow.*

*This afternoon I went for a long walk with Kym, which we both enjoyed. It has been a good day for walking: bitterly cold but fine. Winter seems to be arriving with a vengeance.*

*I wonder if you could send me on a copy of the original of Clive's birth certificate as soon as you get hold of it so that I can produce it here and we can start drawing the extra money.*

*Well sweetheart mine, let's hear from you soon again and tell me everything. Give Clive a big hug from me and keep an extra big one for your darling self.*

*God Bless you, Juanita dearest. Ever Dicky*

#

The commissioning of a new vessel is probably something rarely done more than once in the lifetime of a naval officer, and many never get to experience it during their entire service in the navy. A vessel is decommissioned whenever it is undergoing repairs for a long period or is laid up out of service for any reason. Whether the vessel is new or old, commissioning means getting a new crew. I had plenty of time to plan how I would carry out my responsibilities on board as I had been with the vessel since she had been launched almost two months earlier on May 29, 1941.

The *Whitehaven* was formally commissioned on November 14. Commissioning a new vessel for service during warfare left me with a very strong expectation that I would probably get many crewmembers who had never been to sea in their lives before. *HMS Whitehaven* was a minute cog in the enormous engine that is the Royal Navy. She probably didn't rate experienced crewmembers to man her very light armament and other devices such as sonar, which were virtually unknown in previous wars. Then I suddenly realized that I was probably one of the most inexperienced members of the crew aboard a vessel whose main duty was sweeping mines with equipment I had never seen before. The gunnery course I had undertaken two years previously did not include any information on the enormously powerful windlasses—devices used to raise and lower an anchor and other heavy—being fitted on the after-deck of the *Whitehaven*. Nor were the basics of moored mine-sweeping ever mentioned much less the equipment I was going to be responsible for. I need not have worried because I was about to enter into a period of commissioning called *working up*. I had heard alarming stories about that process, and it was probably just as well because it proved to be excessively alarming.

#

After our sea-trials were successfully completed and the vessel was accepted from the builders, we were off to Tobermory, a port in the Western Isles of Scotland. It was there that all auxiliary vessels of the Royal Navy do their working up. Before leaving, I arranged for Joan and Clive to accept my sister Kathleen's kind invitation to take them into her home at Gullane, a seaside resort about ten miles outside of Edinburgh, Scotland. Gullane was where I had spent several happy days with Hamish and Aunt Ella while on holiday from Haileybury.

I do not recall the exact date when Kathleen and Hamish were married. But I do know that their kindness in helping Joan during my absences abroad during World War II, both before and after Clive was born, made our separation during those terrible years so much easier.

The man in charge of the base at Tobermory was Commodore Stephenson who made sure every vessel that completed the four weeks of working up had a crew completely capable of doing their duties. When a vessel arrived, it requested a berth, anchorages where the vessels stayed for the period of work up. Apparently, it was not unusual for the Commodore to assign a berth that was already occupied or on a shoal and then wait to see whether the captain of the vessel would comply or object.

Heaven help you if you didn't object smartly!

I had also heard that Commodore Stephenson sent orders at any time of the day or night and expected immediate compliance. Allegedly on one occasion, he ordered that two hot breakfast meals consisting of porridge, bacon, eggs, and coffee be sent immediately under oars to his office. At 2 am!

We arrived at Tobermory on December 15, 1941, a week after the attack on Pearl Harbor. Commodore Stephenson never allowed us to forget the need for vigilance. Fortunately, we were never subjected to any really bizarre maneuvers, but on Christmas Day was when the cutter races between all vessels in port took place. Cutters are manned by eight oarsmen and the temperature that day was just a degree or two above freezing.

On another evening, we had to land a platoon on the beach and attack an enemy force somewhere in the woods. All the maneuvers required the presence of officers from vessels, particularly the executive officer. I was ready for bed very early each day. Though there was no time to actually train with our minesweeping equipment, I soon became very acquainted with the procedures.

The *Whitehaven* was then sent to Rosyth, which was on the other side of the Firth of Forth inlet from Gullane; it was great that Joan and Clive were so near, even more so when we received the news that the ship was to be fitted out for service in the Mediterranean. Our new captain was equally happy that the fitting out was to be at Rosyth, which was close to his home at Musselburgh.

The fitting-out process took about two months. Up until then, our ship was known as a J121. During Warship Week in February 1942, it was named *HMS Whitehaven* after the ship and its crew was formally adopted by the West Cumbrian town of Whitehaven. The borough's coat of arms with the motto *Consilio Absit Discordia* (conciliation without discord) was displayed on its quarterdeck.

In late February, we moved from Rosyth to Greenock, back on the west coast of Scotland. It was from there that we finally left for the Mediterranean on March 3, 1942. I am no good at saying goodbyes at the best of times—if that time can ever be described as good. There are occasions, however, when my guardian angel has made it easier for me even though the circumstances have been so sad. This was one when I was allowed a chance to see how well-off I was, compared to the fate that befell some naval service friends.

While we were at Rosyth, I had the great pleasure of meeting officers of other small naval craft also fitting out there. I knew that many of those vessels were fitting out for service in the Baltic in support of convoys destined for Murmansk to help Russia in her struggle against Hitler's eastern campaign. While their vessels were embarking equipment to endure the expected freezing Russian conditions, the *Whitehaven* was embarking awnings to protect us from the Mediterranean sun. Moreover, I'm sure that many crew members of those vessels also had wives and new-born children. The difference was their chances of survival in Russia were much less than those of the *HMS Whitehaven*.

It was a cold March morning when we left Glasgow for Alexandria, Egypt. There were nine vessels in our flotilla. The *HMS Whitehaven,* with George Walter Alexander Thomas Irvine in command, was the vice-leader. The flotilla leader and two vessels had sailed a week before we did and took the same route. We sailed independently of the other vessels.

The weather forecast was not good for the Atlantic Ocean, with gale winds expected throughout the route area we were traveling to Ponta Delgada in the Azores. Since there was no possibility of entering the Mediterranean at the Straits of Gibraltar because of Hitler's dominance there, our only alternative was via the Cape of Good Hope in Africa and then to the Persian Gulf via Mombasa, Kenya, and Aden. Our vessel, being relatively small, would require refueling at least seven times before reaching our final destination.

South of the Scilly Islands, which are located off the southwest tip of Britain, the weather turned ferocious and became a much more formidable enemy for our vessel than anything Hitler could muster. A south-west gale knocked our speed down to about five knots (six mph), which prolonged the agony of bucking seas and mountainous waves doing their utmost to swamp us.

While on the bridge, my thoughts flashed back to the relative comfort of the 6,000-ton cargo vessels I had experienced such gales on during my eight years of passages made in peacetime. This motion was hard to describe, and my heart went out to the young crew members who had to do their duties as best they could with buckets placed in strategic places nearby. To this day, I can see the crewman at the helm trying to maintain the vessel on course and the ASDIC (anti-submarine detection sonar) operator listening for the presence of submarines all the while wishing that they could somehow end the torture. The dank, airless engine room had about two feet of water sloshing around the feet of those on watch.

From Mombasa, we went to Aden for refueling. Our passage through the Red Sea and the Suez Canal was without incident. I had never been through that canal before and could not avoid making a comparison with the other great canal at Panama through which I had crossed about 15 times. The arid surroundings and the lack of locks were in sharp contrast with the lush, tropical countryside, and the three large lock groups at Panama.

When we arrived at Port Said, we received the sobering news that our flotilla leader had been sunk with the loss of her whole crew when she struck a German mine in the port of Mersa Matruh in Egypt. That vessel had arrived at Alexandria about three weeks earlier, and we had been looking forward to working with her in support of the British campaign in North Africa. Now, we became leaders of the Fourteenth Minesweeping Flotilla. George Irvine was promoted to its command. We embarked a doctor as part of his staff, and I became the staff officer of operations.

There was no need for minesweeping while the Allied Eighth Army was struggling to keep Rommel out of Cairo. Things were looking very bleak as the Egyptian ports in North Africa changed hands. While that was happening, we were given the duty of acting as a convoy escort for neutral vessels trading from Port Said northward to Turkish territorial waters off Iskanderun in Anatolia.

This was something new for the *Whitehaven*. The cargo vessels we were to escort were of several nationalities with Greek, Syrian, and Turkish amongst them. Before each convoy sailed, we held the usual conference in Port Said and explained how we expected the ships not to straggle and to always have an officer on watch or nearby who could decipher our International Code flag signals. Those conferences always ended with George Irvine naming the vessel to be convoy commodore. That always went to the captain with the best command of English.

We made several journeys to-and-fro with those neutral ships. Only once did the *Whitehaven* come under attack. That was on a southbound journey off the island of Cyprus. We averted the torpedoes aimed at us rather haphazardly by two Italian aircraft, but I think it did us good to receive concrete proof that a beautiful sunny morning might at any moment turn into a disaster.

While we were engaged in that escort work, Rommel's attacks were having success, and artillery fire could be heard at times in Alexandria. The order came to prepare to abandon the port, and we were to give all possible assistance. We made several trips between Alexandria and Port Said with all sorts of office supplies, which were brought alongside the vessel for evacuation. I believe we were actually the last vessel to leave Alexandria.

We waited in Port Said for further orders, and those soon came. We were to patrol the approaches to Alexandria by night. We were well-equipped with the latest sonar to do that. The concern was that an invasion of Alexandria might be made starting with submarine and motor torpedo boat attacks. Our very light draft made us almost immune from the latter dangers. But I recall the tension we all felt patrolling Alexandria's port before returning to Port Said at daybreak.

History books are full of the ways in which the fortunes of war turned in favor of the British Eighth Army shortly after General Montgomery was put in charge of operations against Rommel. I have always felt sorry for Generals Wavell, Alexander, and Richie who had reduced the strength of the German forces so that Rommel was finally prompted to make the big mistake of overextending his supply lines at Alamein. As we now know, that battle on Cairo's doorsteps turned the war in Africa in favor of the Allies. It also started our minesweeping operations in support of the Eighth Army as they advanced to Tripoli, Libya, reputed to be the longest ever undertaken by a minesweeping force.

We started to sweep with a vengeance. Simply put, our duty was to make sure that supplies could reach the Eighth Army by sea whenever they needed them. This meant that we often swept in an area of the coast that was behind the enemy lines so that as the Germans retreated further, supplies were awaiting the advancing Eighth Army. That there were no highways in the desert and even if there had been, the sea was the safest way to ensure supplies, provided the ports were clear of obstacles such as mines.

Minesweeping for moored mines is much more laborious than pushing a 400 toil magnet before you to detonate magnetic mines. We had to tow knives fitted to wires behind our vessels. The knives are kept outside of the minesweeper's course by kites, and they are kept from sinking too far down by buoyant floats attached to the wires.

The most important piece of the equipment apart from the knife was the kite. Towed correctly, the speed of the vessel will push the knife outwards about 25 yards, meaning that's the width of the area covered with each sweep. If two vessels are utilized, they sweep one behind the other, with the rear vessel keeping the front vessel's float slightly on its left, or port side. That ensures the rear vessel is proceeding in water swept by the leader. Between them, they are sweeping a channel about 50 yards wide. With four vessels, a channel about a 100 yards wide can be swept. When a mine's mooring line is severed, the mine pops up to the surface and is disposed of by rifle fire.

The mines could really be anywhere where the enemy wished to prevent supplies from reaching the Eighth Army by sea, so our sweeping to Tripoli took a month to assure that the approaches to each of the ports were clear. In our favor was that the enemy was leaving each port area as rapidly as possible and the Germans' time was spent getting their land-based equipment back rather than minelaying. Even so, it was imperative there be no repetition of the disaster that had befallen our flotilla leader back at Mersa Matruh at the beginning of this deployment.

When we were finally in possession of the port at Tripoli, we were most pleasantly surprised to learn Winston Churchill was there and would be coming to the minesweeping flotilla anchored outside as a gesture of appreciation for our help in the North African campaign. There was no time to arrange a reception, but we all lined the rails and gave three hearty cheers as his launch passed close to each of our ships.

#

It was most unfortunate for me to suffer from an ailment they say often afflicts tall people. During the latter stages of our sweeping operations, I started to lose blood from enlarged hemorrhoids, so much so that I had to apply the appropriate bandaging.

As a flotilla leader, we had a doctor aboard, and he insisted that on arrival at Malta where we were due to refuel shortly, I should see a doctor. In those days, the island of Malta, located between Tunisia and Sicily, was enduring daily attacks from enemy bases in Italy, and the islanders there were suffering all sorts of deprivation due to continuous attacks on supply-ship convoys and their escorts.

Malta was the largest British naval base in the Mediterranean, and Hitler intended to keep it from being effective in any way. Thanks to the bravery of the islanders, he failed. Our naval vessels could count on fuel supplies throughout the rest of the war, one of the factors that assisted our campaign in Italy when the allied forces invaded Sicily a few months later. Malta was later granted the George Cross, the highest civil decoration given for bravery.

Our call at Malta was for fuel and supplies and provided me medical attention for a complaint that would never improve without surgery—so stated Colonel Mitchell, the Canadian army surgeon at the Malta General Hospital. Recuperation from the hemorrhoidectomy would take two weeks. So the *Whitehaven* sailed on without me.

I will not dwell on the painful aftermath of that surgery, but it was most successful. And the availability of seating on circular cushions was so helpful while I awaited the availability of airspace to rejoin the *Whitehaven*.

There was a minesweeping flotilla at Malta that was particularly active during that long period when Hitler threw everything at the island trying to obliterate it as a very painful thorn in his side. The flotilla leader of that minesweeping force was the *HMS Speedy*, a much larger vessel than the *Whitehaven*. I was most surprised when I was instructed to relieve the captain of that vessel for a week because he'd had no leave for some considerable time—meaning I became captain. I do not recall exactly how this came about, but I was most grateful for the chance to be in charge of sweeping from the bridge of this fine vessel. We left port daily and returned before dark, and I had a ball. I was sad to leave Malta but very happy to be back with Captain George Irvine on the *Whitehaven*.

The landing of US forces in Algeria and the complete domination of the German forces in North Africa clearly meant that the time was ripe for an invasion of Italy via Sicily. Once again, the *Whitehaven* was to lead the minesweeping force ahead of the assault craft and heavy units commanded by General Montgomery who was on the headquarters ship, which was none other than dear old *MV Reina del Pacifico*. There she was in the gray dawn of July 10, 1943, standing out among the less definable naval armada.

As we approached the island of Sicily, through the gloom we could discern the entrance to the port of Syracuse, which was to be the base of operations for the invading force until the whole island was in our hands. As the leading vessel, we were in a good position for a firsthand view of the enemy's reaction to this invasion. Since our duties were to alert the fleet regarding the presence of mines or other defensive measures, we soon found ourselves at the port entrance where we were instructed to stand clear of the invading forces by returning seaward. Shortly after, we became aware of considerable gunfire. We were ultimately ordered back to our base at Alexandria. This meant our services were not required in Sicily, which soon fell. But the invasion of the Italian mainland which was to follow resulted in bloody struggles on the mainland beaches and heavy losses of life.

In November 1942, the United States invaded North Africa and completed the defeat of Rommel's forces on that continent. Without that, the invasion of Sicily in September 1943 would not have been possible. The Mediterranean was now open for commercial traffic once again. When we returned to Alexandria, I learned the navy was sending relief, so I could return to the UK and take the navigator's specialization course I had applied for a year or so earlier. That was good news indeed.

My relief duly embarked in Alexandria, and we went to sea for his indoctrination procedure. While on that last trip, George asked if I would like to leave the ship when we were in Alexandria or would I prefer transferring while at sea to a South African Navy trawler that was returning to Tripoli then find my own way home from there. I jumped at the opportunity to avoid the possibility of naval authorities grabbing me in Alexandria to do local work while awaiting the next westbound convoy to the UK as had been the fate of an acquaintance.

So one bright, sunny morning, the whaler was lowered at sea and eight of the seamen I had spent so much time with on the *Whitehaven* rowed me and my meager belongings over to the trawler. I remember so well the three cheers the whole *Whitehaven* crew gave me as we pulled away from her. I never met up with George Irvine again. However, I heard that he was in command of a minesweeping flotilla operating ahead of invasion forces on D-day during the Normandy invasion.

The next few weeks took me from Tripoli to Liverpool via the unusual means of Libyan cargo vessels to Sfax in Tunisia then by Moroccan vessel to Bizerte in Tunisia then by British Army truck to Algiers then by escort destroyer to Liverpool.

The captains of the two cargo vessels were most hospitable. One of them only traveled by night, adding about two days to my traveling time. The truck from Bizerta to Algiers was luck; oxygen tubes were needed in Algiers that day. As we came over the hill south of Algiers, I could once again see the *Reina del Pacifico* lying at anchor in the bay, and I knew that my luck was in for a faster than usual berth in a high-speed convoy if I could only get down to the naval authorities in Algiers and stake my claim. The truck driver was very accommodating and gave me priority over delivering the oxygen tubes.

When I arrived breathless at the naval headquarters and inquired about a possible berth on any of the vessels of the convoy, I was informed that all the escorts were already at sea patrolling because the convoy was due to sail in about ten minutes.

I was on my dejected way out when one of the officers said the magic words: "Just a minute."

As I came to a screeching halt, he turned to another officer and spoke quietly. Turns out someone had sabotaged one of the escort destroyers by mixing water with the fuel oil. I soon found myself aboard the sabotaged vessel, the *HMS Evinrude*, which was refueling and due to sail within six hours or so. She was of very new construction, and the lieutenant-commander captain was very happy to take me aboard—provided I was willing to keep a watch. I jumped at the chance and was shown to my cabin.

What luck!

We watched the convoy leave, the *Reina del Pacifico* carrying General Montgomery and his staff back to England, the campaign of the Eighth Army in North Africa completed. The speed of the convoy was to be 15 knots (17 mph), which meant that they would be 90 miles ahead of us by the time we sailed from Algiers. I calculated that by steaming at 20 knots, we should catch the convoy up before their arrival in the UK, wherever port that might be. Up till then, one escort vessel would be missing.

The journey home passed without event, and we caught up with the convoy as planned. We left the convoy at the port of Greenock in the Firth of Clyde, an inlet off the southwest coast of Scotland. I thought back a year and a half to the day we left. Our outward journey had taken us about three months. My return journey to the UK was made in about eight days.

After depositing the convoy at Greenock, the captain asked me to take the *Evinrude* to Liverpool where it was due to refuel. He had been on his feet for about 12 hours and wanted a break. He asked me to call him when we were at the pilot station. This was a nighttime passage through the Irish Sea, past the Isle of Man, to the estuary of the Mersey. The visibility was not good enough to see the lighthouses near Anglesey, an island on the north coast of Wales. It was a pitch-black night, so I would have to rely on the radar operator for the most hazardous part of the journey: turning 90 degrees into the Mersey estuary. I asked him to tell me when we were 15 miles away from the Skerries, a group of rocky inlets, near Anglesey.

I waited and waited until I sensed that something was wrong. I dashed into the chart house where the radar was operated and looked at the chart and the radar bearings and distances. I saw that the operator had given me the distance from the highland behind the Skerries. The Skerries was much closer; they were right ahead of us but quite invisible. I immediately ordered the course change 90 degrees to port.

Once again, I had to thank my guardian angel when I woke the captain to tell him that the pilot boat for Liverpool was in sight right ahead of us.

#

While I was away in the Mediterranean, Joan and Clive had moved from Scotland to Chichester in Sussex on the south coast of England after a kind invitation from a brother naval officer and his wife, Colin and Rita Shand. They knew that Joan was going to be on her own for a considerable time, and since Colin—also a navigation specialist—was also slated for foreign service, it was hoped the two ladies would together weather the separation from their husbands.

Actually, things turned out differently.

When visitors came for meals, Joan found herself being denied the use of common areas like the sitting room along with other isolating experiences. When I returned, we lost no time in looking for other living quarters. And there, we were very lucky. The little township of Havant is a dormitory for many people working at Portsmouth, England's largest naval base, which is about five miles away. We decided to look there since I would be commuting to the nautical school while preparing for the navigator's examination. We responded to a listing in the local newspaper from a Miss Austen who was offering a two-bedroom flat with a sitting room, kitchen, and bathroom on the second floor of a late Victorian building. Miss Austen, a spinster lady about 60 years of age, seemed very kind and understanding and her flat upstairs was just what we wanted at a rent that I could afford. So we moved in and started a very happy period in our lives.

One of the happiest events was the birth of our second child, Rodney. I had always rued not being near to Joan when Clive was born in October 1941 because I was the only officer appointed to oversee the fitting out of the *Whitehaven*. Now I was studying at the naval college and living at home in our new digs.

The day was only about two hours old on November 9 when Joan woke me to suggest I should call an ambulance. The ambulances were on wartime alert for air raids, so I knew when I called them that we should be ready as soon as we could. My phoning woke up Miss Austen, and she called up from the foot of the stairs to ask if we would like a cup of tea. In England, the drinking of tea ensures that any important event that it accompanies will be a great success. I thanked Miss Austen profusely but was forced to tell her we didn't have the time. A few minutes after our slow progress down the stair, the ambulance arrived.

Outside, it was a frosty, brightly moonlit night without a cloud in the sky. Joan and I sat in the back of the ambulance. She held onto the stanchion supporting one of the bunks, suffering occasional small pains.

Our road to the nursing home crossed the main London/Portsmouth railroad at a level crossing. As we approached it, to my horror I heard the alarm bell announcing that the gates were closing to allow what had to be the world's longest freight train in the world to pass. That was a bad 15 minutes. Once we were back on our way, I wondered if that child could possibly wait another few minutes while we sped toward the nursing home.

He did. But only just.

The nurse who opened the door calmly took Joan's arm and before closing the door, told me to phone in the morning. I didn't sleep much. When I made that phone call, a voice said that Joan had delivered a healthy boy at about 3:30 am—half an hour after I left the nursing home.

#

During our time in Havant, there were many air raids. All landlords who rented living quarters in the UK during wartime had to supply their occupants with an adequate air-raid shelter away from the house. Miss Austen's was at the back of the house at the far end of her yard. However, Joan and I preferred to share the space under the stairs which had been reinforced to provide another shelter area approved by the authorities. Miss Austen and her aunt, Miss Longley, did not object, so we spent many hours in that space with those two elderly ladies and our two young children. Miss Longley was a particularly young person even though she was 80 years of age.

The first night when the air raid sirens sounded, Miss Austen was very worried because Miss Longley did not come out of her room for some time. Miss Austen finally went to find out what the delay was. She soon came back to our place under the stairs and whispered that Miss Longley was taking all the curlers out of her hair before appearing because "the commander will be with us."

Joan got a kick out of that.

Many things happened while we were at Miss Austen's. It was from there that I had to bid farewell to leave for the invasion of Normandy. And it was there that Miss Austen came upstairs to be with Joan when she read the notification informing her I had been injured in Normandy. It was there that Miss Austen prepared a delicious Christmas lunch I had to dash away from to catch a train for the first leg of my journey around South America after the invasion of Normandy.

Such pleasant memories of kindness received made our final departure from Miss Austen a sad event even though the war was then over.

# Chapter Fourteen
## D-Day

I received my appointment as an officer and navigator with Captain Dolphin, the commanding officer of Group G3, on December 1, 1943. Our headquarters was in Ashley Gardens, Victoria, in London, where I met Captain Dolphin and Lieutenant-Commander Hubert Fox, his staff officer of operations. Once again, I struck lucky with people I worked under.

As navigator, the first thing I did was to obtain a full set of charts covering the English Channel between Southampton and the coast of France and read all the information that pertained to the courses we were to follow to reach Gold Beach, our destination close to the port of Arromanches in Normandy. There did not seem much more I could usefully do after I had satisfied myself that everything was cut and dried from a navigating point of view. After reading all the information at our disposal regarding the invasion of beaches by British and Canadian troops, it was clear what we could expect from the rest of our navy and the Royal Air Force.

It was very clear that air superiority was pivotal before anything else. The British and US Air Forces had been plastering German and French cities for many weeks with great success, completely dominating Goering's Luftwaffe. That made it possible to land troops by parachute and glider behind the German coastal batteries during the original assault across the beaches. While that was going on, the big guns of both countries battleships would plaster the coastal batteries. In the peaceful surroundings of Ashley Gardens, I had difficulty imagining what our first assault would sound like as we approached the coast of France.

The only contribution I imagined our little Group G3 could make to assist the first wave of soldiers would be to blow up the deadly obstacles we knew the Germans had placed on the beaches.

Lieutenant-Commander Fox had the bright idea of making a scale model of the Gold Beach area where we would find ourselves on D-Day if all went well. Gold Beach was one of five designated beaches that were used during the D-Day landings. The other four were Sword, Juno, Omaha, and Utah. The information and photographs at our disposal made that possible. So we made several visits to the nearby Army and Navy stores on Victoria Street to obtain the materials we needed to make our papier-mâché replica. That was not only a pleasant activity for both of us but we hoped that it would help us know more about the place, which surely had to be an advantage.

About three months prior to D-Day, we moved our headquarters from Ashley Gardens to Beaulieu Gardens near Southampton. What on earth had we done right to deserve such a great place to work? The Rothschild family owned the property, which was famous for its rhododendrons.

Sometime in the early months of 1944, I received my promotion to Lieutenant-Commander. Then the May 9, 1944, edition of the *London Gazette* reported that His Majesty had awarded me the Distinguished Service Cross for my time aboard the *HMS Whitehaven*.

What a happy prelude to an invasion!

The chronology for D-Day was set. The Mulberry harbors planned to move old merchant vessels traveling under their own engine power to the beach area and then carefully sink them by opening sea valves to form a breakwater. Many of those old vessels had to be moved from ports in Scotland and northern England to ports nearer the invasion coast. This made it necessary for them to start on their journeys two or three days before the planned D-Day.

We left Southampton on the evening of June 5 in an LCIL—landing craft infantry large—with the senior officers of a Canadian battalion and a full load of infantrymen and their equipment. Behind us followed six more LCILs fully loaded. It was a pitch-black night but with good visibility.

Our course was to take us out from Southampton Water past the western end of the Isle of Wight, out to the English Channel, and across to the French coast. As we approached the Calshot Spit light buoy—the spit is a mile-long sand and shingle bank, the light buoy a warning to sailors—located on the southern bank of the open end of Southampton Water on the south coast of England, I was surprised to see the silhouette of a vessel against the lighter eastern sky. Then further ahead, another such silhouette.

This was not what I had expected. No ships should have been coming into Southampton Water on that night. Then I realized what had happened. As I'm sure most people know, D-Day was supposed to happen on June 5 but was moved back a day because of bad weather and gusting winds. But the old ships for the Mulberry harbors had set sail on their originally appointed time to be in place on June 5, and those were the silhouettes I saw.

It was one of the problems we had to expect from moving the invasion to a day later than planned. I knew that there was nothing I could do, but I was very worried about the LCILs astern of us. I was going to pass the incoming ships in a relatively wide part of the channel but the end LCILs would have to pass them in a narrow place I had already passed. I had visions of possible collisions and felt helpless to do anything about it.

On June 6, the naval bombardment at Gold Beach got underway at 05:30 am, with large warships firing at the German coastal batteries. Smaller vessels such as destroyers were patrolling to locate possible submarines. At exactly 7 am, we were off Gold Beach, and the skipper of the LCIL prepared to beach his craft. German shells were visible landing in the water astern of us as we approached the beach.

The amphibious landings commenced at 7:25 am. Once the troops were ashore, it was our turn. Captain Dolphin said he was ready, and we jumped together. As we landed up to our knees, he said, "I was going to take my boots off." It was a long time before I saw him or Hubert Fox again.

I never gave a thought about our papier-mâché model; there was too much else occupying my attention. I felt at a great disadvantage because I really had nothing else to do except staying alive. I knew that if the men we had landed were successful in securing the beachhead, I wouldn't be needed. My revolver stayed in its holster, and I laid low. Surprisingly there was not as much small arms fire as I had expected, and in about an hour, it seemed to subside altogether, presumably because the enemy was being overcome by the first wave of our soldiers. And in fact, the landings at Gold Beach were to prove highly successful.

It must have been about half an hour after reaching the beach that I noticed the first soldier removing the obstacles the Germans had placed on the beaches by laying charges, running to a detonator, then blowing them up. He gladly accepted my offer to do the detonating. So it took an invasion to achieve a long-desired wish I had ever since seeing the first cowboy movie where they pushed a plunger to create a great explosion.

It was not long before I saw the first group of enemy prisoners, very adequately guarded by one of our soldiers. There certainly were not enough yet to create a problem, nor was it possible to transfer them off the beach yet. My intention was to make myself as conspicuous as possible to members of our own armed services, so they would recognize me as someone to whom they might speak if anything was needed.

I walked toward Arromanches, where a port was to be placed, hoping to catch up with any member of my group. I had no sense of the passage of time. It was getting dark when I heard the scream of an aircraft engine and the pinging of machine-gun bullets. By this time, the beach had become a parking lot for every type of armed vehicle including tanks, which was clearly the target this isolated German fighter was seeking.

I dove under one of the tanks for protection but not before I felt a sharp pain in my knee on one leg and my ankle on the other. I thought I had been hit by bullets, but when I tried to turn on my back, I could not move my legs. They were pinned by something.

Soon a man walked up, and as he peered down at me, I heard him say to someone, "I think he's dead."

I reacted violently to show him how mistaken he was and caught a glimpse of what was on me—a passenger-filled army staff car whose occupants must have been of some importance.

"Get off my legs!" I shouted.

That was soon done, and I was relieved to find I could move my legs. That was the signal for the car and its passengers to disappear. The aircraft did not return for another attack, and the anti-aircraft guns had stopped firing. I wondered whether it might have been a mistake to seek the shelter of the tank, but everybody else was diving under some vehicle when the plane dive-attacked us. My only mistake was that I left my long legs in the traffic lane.

Very soon, I knew there was water on that injured knee, and my ankle also started to swell. I'm not sure how long I lay there, but I knew the tablets we took to keep awake before sailing from Southampton were wearing off because I suddenly felt very tired. I had to do something to reduce the pain in my knee. I took out my invasion knife and cut the trouser leg, so it ceased to press on my now very swollen knee. That indeed reduced the pain, and I was able to start crawling away from the tank.

I don't know how long I crawled, but I eventually found a large hole someone had made, and there, I fell asleep. It was daylight when I awoke and with much pain got out of the hole. The first person I saw was our accountant who acted very quickly to get me aboard a hospital ship back to England.

Meanwhile, poor Joan was suffering through what must surely be one of the worst aspects of warfare. Someone delivered an envelope to our address, which Miss Austen received. It was addressed to Mrs. Goodwin and had obviously come from some branch of the admiralty. That was enough for Miss Austen to deliver it personally, no doubt believing it surely must contain bad news.

Kindness, I suppose, is seldom overpowering, and for that reason, I cannot fault our dear landlady's intention of being present when Joan read the message. I do wish so much, however, that she had read the contents before assuming the worst.

As she handed the envelope to Joan, she said, "You must be very strong, dear."

The news, of course, was that Lieutenant-Commander Goodwin had been wounded in the left knee and right ankle and was in a hospital in England. There was no possibility of either of us calling to find out where I was in England. I didn't know until I was released fit for duty about ten days later that it was a hospital in Nottingham.

Back at the beaches and the village of Arromanches, I was delighted to be appointed assistant admiralty berthing officer at the Mulberry Harbor B, which was almost completely in service seaward of Arromanches village. That was where our Group G3 was meant to be right at the start.

I was pleased to hear I was the only one who had gotten there via Nottingham.

I soon found accommodations at a French farmhouse about two miles from Arromanches and was given a motorcycle. Then followed a very happy period of my war effort. The Mulberry Harbor was completely afloat, meaning it rose and fell with the enormous channel tides as much as 26 feet. It only moved vertically with the tide. The horizontal movement of the tidewater as it came in and out of the channel was checked by the spud pontoons hanging on large posts that vessels berthed beside to discharge their cargoes. Those pontoons were positioned about 100 yards seaward of the high tide mark where vessels with drafts of at least 20 feet could berth. Floating pontoons also securely anchored formed roadways along which traffic could go from vessels to the road system ashore. Old vessels were also sunk and helped to act as breakwaters.

My immediate superior was Captain Hickling, later a vice-admiral, who was the naval officer in charge of the Mulberry B. Needless to say, my duties were varied but always interesting as vessels came in steady streams alongside the spud pontoons, off-loaded their vehicles and cargoes, then disappeared over the western horizon to England again.

While there, the weather was mainly good, and things went without a hitch, thanks indeed to the air superiority we had enjoyed ever since D-Day. Our Mulberry would have never been possible if the Germans had any planes to menace us with.

We had many visitors to our harbor; the most imposing was Winston Churchill. He arrived with two or three

Russian generals who were astounded seeing the port working at full capacity, and they went away much happier.

It was now late July 1944, and I was living in a farmhouse about a mile away from Mulberry. I commuted by motorcycle daily and nightly as needed. One morning, Captain Dolphin called me to his office and showed me a signal from the admiralty in London.

*Lieutenant-Commander Goodwin is to report to the NA2SL forthwith for a very important future appointment.*

Dolphin said, "You know, Pilot, this is not wording usually used by their Lordships; someone obviously wants to see you in a hurry."

I knew what he said was true. As soon as I gathered my bits and pieces, he gave me the use of an MTB, which got me to Plymouth at 25 knots (29 mph). From there, I caught the first train for London and a taxi to the admiralty.

As I sat in the waiting room, I wondered what on earth—or elsewhere—my services were being sought for. After about 20 minutes, the door to the inner office opened and out came the naval assistant to the Second Sea Lord. He was a retired rear admiral and was holding some papers.

He said, "I understand you speak Spanish."

I told him I had not used the language at all for about four years.

He went onto explain how in peacetime, it was an admiralty policy to *show the flag* by sending a naval destroyer or cruiser to visit countries both in and outside the Commonwealth. Wartime had prohibited all that, but now the admiralty had charged the Ministry of Information to find an officer with active war service in the navy to visit countries in South America and talk about the work that he and the navy had been doing.

He asked me if I would like to be considered for that work.

I said that I would.

He gave me papers to take to Lieutenant-Commander Schorr at Whitehall, so he could put my name on the list for that duty.

At Whitehall, I felt more at ease because I was speaking to someone of equal rank. After Schorr described details of the work I'd be expected to do, I asked him about the list that I had agreed should now have my name on it. He said that my name was the only one on it! That made things even easier, and I felt free to ask a host of questions.

I found out that Schorr had been a schoolmaster at a British school in Montevideo, Uruguay. To find out how good my Spanish was, he arranged a lunch with the Chilean naval attaché at the RAC Club, so he could listen to the conversation because he knew that Captain Gilmore's English was not very good.

So the next day at 1 pm, we were at the RAC club bar, and I discovered Captain Gilmore was trying to improve his English by practicing it on us. So for about half an hour before we went to the dining room, there was something of a competition going on. Gradually, the Spanish language won the day and when at about 4 pm we stood on the sidewalk outside the club after bidding the Chilean attaché goodbye, I asked Schorr about my Spanish.

He said, "You're in."

I was told that the Ministry of Information was going to make the schedule for talks in each of the countries on my tour with the assistance of the press attaché at each British Embassy. Schorr was expecting me to leave on my tour within two weeks; however, when I explained that it would take me at least a month to prepare my lectures and obtain movies and other material, he arranged a desk for me at the Ministry of Information, and I started work there.

I find it hard to describe my reaction to this new work I was suddenly asked to take on. It was clearly an opportunity to prove that I could speak and understand the Spanish language, which was necessary for a successful tour. But it was the impact on my audiences that worried me most, and I tried to get a feel for that imagining myself as an audience member.

I heard that an RAF officer had already made a similar tour of South America and had been very successful. I had no reason to doubt that any officer in any of the armed forces who had been on active duty would be a success with any audience before even uttering a word. Obviously, something more than that was needed to achieve true self-satisfaction, and I soon concluded that it would be my experience of warfare from the point of view of any housewife or householder in any city, town, or village in England that would be of greater interest to their South American counterparts than any military or naval action I had partaken in.

This was the first World War where civilians had contributed so much to victory. Had I been subjected to those risks in the company of my wife and other civilians just so I could give a firsthand account of how it felt?

I don't know, but I was resolved to believe that the answer to both questions was a resounding yes.

# Chapter Fifteen
# On Tour

I found my schedule of talks was often extended, which I took as a compliment. In Panama, I happily complied with a request from the general in charge of the US forces there to give a talk in Spanish to the Puerto Rican infantrymen. Thanks to a plane lent to me by the US Army, I was able to comply with that additional commitment, which brought the total number of talks to 16 in six days. Everything went without a hitch throughout the itinerary. I traveled in the only planes available in those days, DC3s, and from Panama went to Cuba, Venezuela, Colombia, Ecuador, Peru, Chile, Argentina, Brazil, and Mexico City.

It was only in Cuba that I had any trouble. Wing Commander Devey, the British Air attaché stationed in Panama, accompanied me to Havana because it was in his territory. For reasons unknown to me, we missed the plane to Caracas. Hasty calls to the airlines found a connection to Caracas that would arrive in time to prevent upsetting arrangements already made. We just had to make it to Camaguey, a town in the interior of Cuba, by 7 pm that evening.

Devey's connections with the Cuban military authorities proved to be of great use. He told me that the Cuban Airforce had well-kept fighter aircraft as trainers, and he thought that he could arrange to use those planes to get us to Camaguey. Happily, Cuba was a great democratic country in those days under President Batista. During my stay in Havana, I had a pleasant meeting with him and the head of the Cuban Air Force, the same man who approved our request for air transportation to Camaguey without hesitation—even though we needed three fighter planes: one for Devey, one for me, and one for our baggage.

So we flew in formation to Camaguey and made our connection, which saved the day in Caracas. I have had a very soft spot in my heart for President Batista and his staff ever since. What a wonderful place Cuba was in those days.

#

It took me a little time to come to terms with my duties in Latin America. The historical events I was talking about were generally well-known because they had been covered in the daily press, although without much detail. And in many cases, I could not add that detail for obvious reasons of secrecy. I wondered whether my presence would only have its attraction because I was a survivor of those incidents and not a purveyor of the interesting details.

I certainly need not have worried. My accounts of detonating magnetic mines and mine-sweeping in support of the Eighth Army's advance in North Africa, the invasions of Sicily and Normandy, and the heroic resistance of the British civilians that led to the decisive victory at the Battle of Britain, held my audience's attention because they knew I had been there personally.

In Chile were Joan's parents and personal friends who had not seen her since she sailed away in November 1939 to marry me and became one of London's bravest of the brave during the Battle of Britain. My itinerary included two weeks vacation in Chile. Obviously, someone knew of my connections with that country. The press secretary at the British Embassy was a personal friend of Joan; they had worked together at the embassy in the years just prior to the war. So when I was given the assignment, the admiralty said Joan would be welcome to accompany me if I wished. Of course, I wished, but it was simply not possible for obvious family reasons.

As you can imagine, for me Chile was the highlight of the tour. So much had happened since I last saw my dear in-laws, Judith and Bill Gamon. They had purchased a retirement home in the town of Llifen on the eastern end of Lake Ranco in the south of Chile. I knew they'd had some qualms about making that decision because Judith had a history of kidney trouble and related surgeries, which would shorten her life. They were keen for me to see the place, and I was more than keen to take them up on the offer. So as soon as I reached Santiago, they made the necessary arrangements for me to visit Llifen, which meant being down there for about ten days.

#

*My siblings and I have been considering a visit to the beautiful area of Chile called Llifen. Interestingly, in*

136

*looking for more information, an exchange of correspondence took place between Sylvia and a Miguel Proboste Ziegler of Fundo Chollinco Lodge. It turns out that he is the grandson of Miguel Ziegler who owned the lodge when our father was passing through to stay with his in-laws, the Gamons. He lent a horse to our father! Ziegler senior sold the house that the Gamons owned at the time.*

*In the latest correspondence, the grandson was amazed to learn of our connection to his grandfather and commented (translated from Spanish): "What a pleasure to know about you, old friends of the family who lived in these parts of the country so many years ago and knew my grandfather."*

*The grandson informed us that they own the lodge (http://www.hosteriachollinco.cl) and were repairing it.*

— *Rodney*

#

I took the night sleeper train from Santiago to La Union, arriving there at about 1 pm and soon realized that all the main amenities for visitors such as hotel accommodation and transportation were controlled by members of the German/Chilean colony. Before my visit was over, I wished that I knew German to understand what people were saying; however, in my presence, they were all most courteous.

The day after my arrival I took the bus to a hotel at the western end of Lake Ranco. It was almost dark when I reached it, but the owner and his wife were expecting me. She advised me that her husband would be back soon with my supper—freshly caught fish. That meal was most certainly worth waiting for.

I was told that the ferry to Llifen would not arrive before 2 pm the next day, so it was arranged that I go fishing after breakfast. I went out in a rowing boat manned by a young Chilean boy about 16 years of age. My stay in the south of Chile did not leave me much time for delays, and I already felt a day late because I had arrived too late for the previous day's ferry. So it was an unpleasant surprise to see the ferry arriving at the hotel pier at about 11 am. I asked my companion, somewhat abruptly no doubt, why it was so early. He reassured me that it stayed there for lunch and left at about 2 pm. Stupid me believed that until about half an hour later when I saw the ferry leaving.

I reeled in my line and told the young Chilean that I wanted to go back to the hotel right away, and since there was no ferry until tomorrow, I would go to the port of Ranco on the south side of the lake on horseback and catch the same ferry before it left there for Llifen about 4 pm.

He said all that would be possible.

I said goodbye to my lunch and mounted one of the horses while my ex-fishing companion mounted the other, holding my suitcase in front of him on the pommel of his saddle. And so off we went to Ranco.

It turned out to be quite a ride. The river was crossed on a wooden flat barge, and from there the lake disappeared from view behind some of the largest blackberry bushes I had ever seen, bearing some of the largest blackberries that were just ripe. That was the only time I considered it was worthwhile to stop and reach that fruit without dismounting.

Something had to replace my lunch, and my companion seemed amused that I was hungry.

At last, the lake appeared again, and the pier at Ranco became visible. We hastened the pace and galloped into Ranco as the ferry siren sounded. I jumped off the horse and onto the boat as the mooring lines were being taken in. I breathed a sigh of relief that the hotel owner and his 16-year-old partner in crime did not get my board and lodging for another day although the income was replaced by the horse rental.

#

Llifen was a delightful place. Obviously, the most important man in the neighborhood was Mr. Ziegler. It was from that German/Chilean gentleman that Ma and Pa Gamon had bought their house and land. I settled into my room, and since it was still daylight, I wanted to comply with an errand my in-laws had requested. They asked if I could return an alarm clock they had repaired in Santiago to its owner, Count von Reichenbach, at his house near Llifen.

I asked Ziegler where the Reichenbachs lived and he waved his hand eastward and said the house was about three miles away. Apparently, there was only a track to the Reichenbach's property, but since there was still an hour of daylight, I decided to run my errand then and there.

Ziegler offered me a horse and either a British or a Chilean saddle; he was not surprised when I chose the former. So off I went with the alarm clock, galloping eastward toward the mountains through woodland, which made the scenery more somber even though the sun had not yet set. Quite suddenly, my steed came to an abrupt stop with a few snorts that I knew indicated fear. I could see nothing near us. About 20 yards away to the left of the track were the roots of a fallen tree. I tried to urge the horse forward with no luck; clearly, the horse did not want to go anywhere near the fallen tree. So I dismounted, gathered the bridle and reins, and walked with him well into the woods to the right of the track to lose sight of the tree. Once we were far enough away, I returned to meet the track, remounted, and continued.

About half an hour later, when it was getting quite dark, I sighted the Reichenbachs' house, which Ziegler had told me would be the only place I would see before the track ended. Ziegler had also phoned to tell them I was on the way. They were very hospitable and insisted I stay the night, which comforted me a little. When I expressed worry about the horse, they laughingly told me that Chilean horses did not work overtime. As soon as he was unsaddled, Mrs. Reichenbach gave him a slap on the rump and sent him to pasture for the night. That was the beginning of a very pleasant evening, a great dinner, and a sound sleep I badly needed—my posterior was complaining about the excessive time it had spent on the backs of two horses.

The Reichenbachs were a most interesting couple. He had been a wealthy and aristocratic member of the Berlin society before Hitler. He attended Oxford University and while there had made friends with members of English society about whom he had many anecdotes. It seemed that he had made many visits to England and was a keen golfer, which he used to safeguard his wealth by buying banknotes he smuggled into England in the hollow shafts of his golf clubs.

I think it was Bill Gamon who told me that Mrs. Reichenbach was Jewish and that was undoubtedly the reason for their travels outside Germany prior to 1938. The count told me that they had been all over the world, looking for the place they would settle when they retired from travel. They decided to stay in Llifen.

After breakfast the next morning, we strolled around their estate. Apparently, there was a considerable difference in their ages, and it was Mrs. Reichenbach who did most of the heavy work around the house and with their considerable hens and ducks. Her husband had heart trouble, which restricted him to reading English novels as his chief pastime. They had built their house at the foot of a mountain, and their property extended up and over the top of it. The count said a lake up there was his property too, but he had had no way of checking because his health prevented him from wandering too far from the house. I would have happily stayed longer with those kind people, but I did have a deadline for my return to Santiago, and there was always that ferry to cope with!

On my horseback ride back to Llifen, I completely forgot to look for the large, uprooted tree and my horse did likewise. Possibly during daylight hours, something about it was less menacing to him.

It's strange how incidents in our lives can sometimes be connected even though they occur years and miles apart. About 55 years after my visit to the Reichenbachs' home, along that dark track in the south of Chile, I visited my sister Kathleen at Wimbledon. Her leg neuropathy had just started, so she was unable to enjoy the great walks we used to have on Wimbledon common. One day, she wanted to show me something on the common she had never seen before. It was a bee's nest, which had attracted all nature lovers who frequented that beautiful part of Wimbledon. We drove up there, and I parked the car close to our destination, so the walk was a short one.

Then there it was; the roots of an enormous tree that had blown down in a gale. When we got close, I could see that the earth stuck to the roots was still moist and a light-gray color. But the most noticeable thing was the mass of bees that were flying around and going in and out of the holes. To my surprise, as soon as I saw the roots at Wimbledon, I thought of that day in riding to the Reichenbach house. Could bees have surrounded the roots of that tree in Chile and that's what frightened the horse? Had that horse been stung at some time and never forgotten it?

My visit to Llifen was all too short. How much I regretted that Joan could not be with me during that time. I was so happy to report to Ma and Pa back in Santiago that I considered them to be one of the luckiest couples because they had a place like Llifen to retire to. It was truly beautiful. Joan and I had often talked about their decision not to return to England or to stay in Santiago or Viña del Mar after Pa retired because of Ma's kidney problems. Joan feared that Llifen might be too far off the beaten track should she require medical aid. But both Joan and I knew they were determined to make Llifen their home as long as it was physically possible. After seeing the place, I certainly could not blame them for their decision and told them so.

Back in circulation on the lecture tour, I had two weeks of talks while in Chile. Ma and Pa were so kind in putting me up at their house. I'm afraid that my visit upset the peace and quiet of their normal lives. The same applied to Mrs. Mae Struthers, Jack's mother, who was also the epitome of kindness. Needless to say, many of Joan's old-time friends were happy to get up-to-date news of her.

The remainder of my tour of duty went well, and some important events occurred during that time. While I was in Santiago, Franklin D. Roosevelt had died. VE Day—the Allied victory in Europe—caught me in Buenos Aires. And my birthday coincided with my visit to Mexico. The embassy staff in Mexico City arranged a very nice little party for me, and two days later, I was on my way to New York.

That was the first time I had ever been in that great city. But with no ties there and no knowledge of its geography, it was not a good time. It was clear that New York had probably never been as full of humanity as was then the case. United States forces were beginning to return from Europe, and their families were going to New York to meet them.

Fortunately, while in Mexico, I met a lady connected with the US embassy there who was in charge of a local house belonging to a wealthy gentleman named Harry Berman. Before leaving Mexico, that lady had asked me to call Mr. Berman while I was in New York and tell him that the house and everything connected with it was in tip-top condition. Since I had visited that home, I could certainly vouch for what the lady said, but I had decided not to call him with such a slender reason for introducing myself.

The *Queen Elizabeth* was due to sail about three days after my arrival in New York. Having time, I tried desperately to buy a theatre ticket for one of the many plays and musicals advertised. The elderly lady at the theatre kiosk in the hotel lobby smiled wryly when I made my first inquiry the evening of my arrival. She had been completely sold out for some time but suggested I give her my room number in case there were any cancellations. It was easy for me to keep in touch with her because I had to pass her kiosk every time I entered or left the hotel, which was frequently since I was determined to see as much of the city as possible, and I always stopped and chatted a while with her.

On the eve of my departure date, I was informed that the *Queen Elizabeth* would be delayed for at least three days, which was bad news for me since I was finding little to do in New York. So I decided to call Mr. Harry Berman at his apartment on Fifth Avenue. He listened as I delivered the message about his house in Cuernavaca, Mexico, then insisted I accept his invitation to lunch at his home that same day at 1 pm. I hoped my gratitude was not too obvious when I accepted.

That meal was one of several kindnesses I received from the Bermans. In the course of lunch served *à trois*, I learned much from Mr. and Mrs. Berman. Naturally, they asked what I had been doing while in New York. They were surprised to hear I had not been to the theater and inquired about my tastes in theatrical entertainment. They announced that two tickets for each of the three most popular shows would arrive at my hotel that afternoon.

I was overcome with genuine gratitude, and the conversation drifted to another subject of great interest to the Bermans: the cinema. Mrs. Berman asked me who my favorite cinema actors and actresses were. I immediately named Joan Fontaine as one.

That was met with an exclamation from Mrs. Berman, "Oh Harry, what a pity the commander wasn't here earlier this morning when Joan and Brian were here!" Turning to me, she said, "You know, Joan Fontaine married Brian Aherne not so long ago."

I would read later that Fontaine and Aherne divorced in June 1945, literally just weeks after this conversation.

It was apparent that the Bermans had close ties with the cinema and theatre. But Harry had acquired his wealth by trading rubber. Mrs. Berman came from a wealthy family. She was the heir to the Kayser Bondor fortune—the company was a well-known global manufacturer of undergarments, particularly hosiery.

The theatre tickets Harry sent me were for the musicals *Carousel* and *The Voice of the Turtle*, and the play *Harvey*. As soon as I received them, I made sure to pass by the lady at the theatre ticket kiosk. I invited her to accompany me to any one of those shows. She was effusive in her thanks and sad when she said there was no way she could be free to keep me company. But she asked if I really wanted to do her a favor. When I assured her that was the case, she asked if I would take her 15-year-old daughter to *Carousel*. I did just that and knew that the young schoolgirl enjoyed her evening as much as I did.

I have to admit that I honestly cannot recall what I did with the extra tickets for the other two shows. I can only recall that of the three shows, I enjoyed *The Voice of the Turtle* the most. But how much more I would have enjoyed everything I did on my whole tour if only Joan could have been with me.

To cut a long story short, in addition to the theater tickets, my extended stay in New York thanks to the *QE's* delay in sailing included a cocktail party in the Bermans' apartment for about 20 guests, two nights at their residence at Princeton, and a shopping expedition at Saks Fifth Avenue with Harry who bought several items of clothing while attended by the store's manager, no less. The only favor they asked of me in return came from Mrs. Berman; she wanted me to deliver some hats in two large boxes to a friend in Mayfair, London. This, I was very pleased to do, of course.

The voyage home on the *QE* was uneventful but interesting from a human point of view. I never thought that I would be sailing at high speed across the Atlantic in the company of human beings whose lives had been exposed to conditions of a world war. All of a sudden, it was as if the director of the movie had shouted "Cut!" and all the actors knew the wild scenes of danger and destruction had now ended and next would be scenes of reconciliation at the happy ending—or so we all hoped.

The passenger list on the *QE* included high-ranking officers of several nationalities as well as a considerable bevy of ladies from the United Nations Relief and Rehabilitation Administration (UNRRA), returning from various theatres of war to their various countries in Europe. I was one of the few British naval officers and certainly as commander the most junior in rank.

The pastimes most evident were card-playing and dancing after dinner. The stage directions for the play stated quite clearly that no passengers were allowed on deck after sunset, presumably aimed at reducing the risk of lights being seen, but more importantly to ensure that this was not to be an X-rated production!

Early during the voyage home, I received a visit from the officer in charge of all British naval personnel aboard. He was a retired Royal Navy captain, and the purpose of his visit was to advise me that the "Up Spirits" bugle call was at 11 am and 6 pm daily. "Up Spirits" was played once daily on ships when rum was issued to ranks other than officers. In the case of the *QE*, rum was replaced by pink gins, and the place of issue was the cabin of this British naval officer in charge.

I was certainly not interested in gambling, but I did attend the issue of pink gins occasionally, chiefly because I met many interesting officers of all ranks there. I also made friends with the *QE's* chief officer and second officer, and we had many interesting chats. On one occasion after dinner, I was walking up and down the main lobby with the second officer, and after a bit, I excused myself to go to my cabin and turn in for the evening. My companion ruefully stated that he would like to do likewise but couldn't for another hour. I asked him why to which he said that his cabin was otherwise occupied!

And so for me, World War II ended. I could not help but look back through the pictures so clearly etched in my mind of the people I shared those war days with. Of course, the images of men who died in the conflict can never fade: schoolboy friends such as Donal Young, an officer in the Black Watch Regiment who was killed in North Africa; Teddy Kingwood killed at Dunkirk in 1940; Sub-Lieutenant

Rogers killed in an air raid on Portsmouth, as well as all those whose names I never got to know who were killed in air raids on London in 1941. Men who were with me one day and gone the next. I am sure that they were given a special place with millions of others of all nations in God's haven of rest and happiness.

Now I had to prepare for peace.

# Chapter Sixteen
# Lobitos, Peru

Once back in England with Joan, Clive, and Rodney, I caught up with all the news I had been so short of since leaving the Christmas lunch six months earlier on December 25, 1944. I was also able to share what I had been doing, and that took several long conversations. In due course, we came to the subject most in our hearts: what were we going to do as soon as I was demobilized?

All my qualifications made me suitable for some occupation connected with ships and shipping. I now had the opportunity to sit for my master's examinations to qualify for duty in the Merchant Marine with the idea of becoming captain of a ship. There it seemed I had good prospects of being hired right away by my previous employers, the Pacific Steam Navigation Company. In retrospect, I had never considered being parted again from my family for long periods except as a last resort. Such a life would have been inevitable if I returned to the PSNC.

During my talking tour in South America, I'd had some conversations with people at cocktail parties. Somehow, talking about my future after the war at those functions seemed so irrelevant to the duties I was performing that I never made a note of them or took them seriously, believing the subject was probably prompted more by alcohol than a sincere interest in my future. But once home, I was genuinely determined to give Joan and my sons a better life. I wanted them to forget the nights spent under the stairs and in cellars dodging enemy bombs. I wanted them to forget what the wail of air raid sirens sounded like.

Shortly after my return from South America, I received a very nice letter from Lobitos Oilfields office in London telling me that based on my visits to Talara and Lobitos in Peru, they had received a letter from Mr. Fred Milne offering me the post of assistant marine superintendent at the Lobitos oilfield, which he represented.

That letter did not immediately have the effect of galvanizing me into replying. It was a very nice conversation piece because I learned from Joan that her parents knew "Uncle" Fred Milne quite well. He was a shareholder of note in Duncan Fox & Co, the firm Joan's father was working for as produce manager in Santiago. I remembered speaking with Mr. Milne in Lima after he had been introduced to me at a cocktail party at the Bolivar Hotel by Mrs. Forbes, the wife of the British Ambassador to Peru. At least I knew with absolute certainty that alcohol had nothing to do with *Tio* Fred's interest in my future.

It made me very happy to note that Joan seemed quite prepared to face life in the Peruvian desert when we discussed the pros and cons involved. I suggested we might try it out since the contract I would sign would only be for three years at a time. The education of our children did not seem to be a problem since, in three years' time, they would barely be of school age. So we decided to write to Lobitos Oilfields and accept the job.

In due course, I was demobilized. I signed the contract, and we embarked on a vessel at Newport in South Wales destined for St Johns, New Brunswick, from where we would travel by train to New York and from there by train to Miami and from there by air to Talara, Peru, where we would be met and transferred by road to Lobitos, located near the Pacific Coast in northern Peru not far from the border with Ecuador.

Our life in Lobitos lasted three years. The oilfield extended east of the coastline about 20 miles then north of the Talara port to a point about 40 miles north of the Lobitos port. That included the port of Cabo Blanco, which was located about 15 miles from Lobitos on the westernmost point of the South American continent. The port was a fishing village that had been supplied with a submarine pipeline, which permitted vessels to secure to buoys to load oil. About a thousand feet immediately above Cabo Blanco was the township of El Alto, reached by a serpentine, mile-long road. El Alto, which had a hospital, was where about half of all the oilfield's employees lived.

The most important aspect of Lobitos Oilfields was the very high quality of its crude oil. That made it feasible from an economic perspective to have the oil from Peru refined in Lancashire, England. It was the by-products from the refined crude that made the transportation possible at a considerable financial benefit. The shareholders, apparently, had a gold mine rather than an oilfield.

The two tankers owned by Lobitos Oilfields made regular trips between Lobitos or Cabo Blanco to Ellesmere

Port on the River Mersey where the refining was done. Near the port of Talara was another port that exported crude and gasoline for a larger oilfield originally owned by Imperial Oil of Canada but subsequently bought out by Standard Oil of New Jersey.

I found out that my duties in Lobitos and Cabo Blanco included everything that could remotely be considered a part of the port administration, from piloting vessels to the maintenance of submarine pipelines as well as the piers themselves. There were no wharves in either of those two ports, so all dry cargo was consigned to Lobitos where it was discharged to barges that docked alongside the small pier fitted with cranes.

Jim Massie, who was the marine superintendent, had been there for several years and was planning to retire. About two months after I arrived, he went on a three-month vacation and left me to myself. One of the duties which was completely new to me was supervising the construction of an extension to the Lobitos pier and fitting it with a crane capable of lifting 15 tons. The cranes there previously could only handle a maximum of five tons.

Jim Massie was a mine of information on the subject of pile driving, and he had trained two Peruvian foremen, originally carpenters, to become experts. However, the final word as to procedure, such as the moment when the driving had been done sufficiently, had to come from me. Then came the reinforcement rods inside the piles and finally the cement mixture around that.

I remember spending a long time on that pier between piloting T2 tanker ships to the buoys in both Lobitos and Cabo Blanco, where I had to spend the night in El Alto while the ship was loading. When she was ready to leave, I again ensured she was cleared from the buoys. Incidentally, I had received a Peruvian pilotage license to do this. So much for my work.

The oil field management was in the hands of Mr. Linton who I had met a year earlier when giving my lectures at Lobitos and El Alto. He was a strange man whose strangeness I could only put down to having a chip on his shoulder. Indeed he could be described as a very well-balanced man in that he had a permanent chip on each shoulder.

He gave me the impression that he permanently sought recognition but gave no indication of how he wished to be recognized. For instance, he was very keen on cricket, and I honestly believe that he wished all his staff to know how well he played that game. I found little time to play in Lobitos, but I noticed that most of the department heads did their best to join in because they would merit brownie points by doing so. I believe that Linton sincerely felt bad about not having taken an active part in World War II, and it irked him that others had. This tended to compensate for his misfortune by overstressing his position as manager.

Our daughter, Stephanie, was born on November 3, 1946. We were so happy. To quote an ancient phrase, our quiver was now full.

When the company doctor diagnosed Stephanie with enteritis, we took her to the hospital in El Alto. There was no accommodation there for parents to stay overnight with their children. If we had known how ill Stephanie was, we would have made arrangements to stay with friends. Had we known many things about the hospital, we would have acted very differently, and we certainly would not have put blind faith in the doctors or their hospital staff.

The day after we visited Stephanie, it was a terrible shock to get a call at my office on the Lobitos pier from the senior doctor to tell us that she had passed away. The cause of death was heart failure, but isn't all death due to that? Nobody could explain what caused that failure. After Stephanie left us, we struggled to find a reason for such a tragedy. We looked hard for reasons in our care for her. What had we done or not done?

Our natural instinct was to ask the Good Lord to grant us another gift, another daughter, and the guidance, if any were needed, to be sure this would not happen again. So many thoughts tortured me. How was it that when I had to stay in El Alto until a tanker sailed in case of an emergency, the company made accommodations available to me? Perhaps if we had only known how ill Stephanie was, they would have made accommodations available to us. Were the doctors at all worried about Stephanie's condition after we left her the day before she died? Nobody gave us any inkling there was cause for worry.

The questions we asked the doctors and nurses and the answers they gave us certainly would never bring Stephanie back to us. Perhaps her case might prevent any other parent in similar conditions to suffer similar sadness. We hoped that some good came out of this case. For us, we had to sadly close the chapter on Stephanie's life and look to another prayer being granted—which it was with the birth of our daughter Sylvia in 1948.

#

*I was about three years old when Stephanie died, and I have a recollection of her very sick in her crib and the family tending to her. I know that for the rest of my father's life, he never spoke of her. It was a sadness that he never overcame, a sense of guilt perhaps. My mother cautioned us as children not to mention her name around him. My sister, Sylvia, only found out about Stephanie many years later when living in Lima.*

*I have a vivid memory of being with my family in Llifen, Chile, going out on the lake to fish, the smell of wood burning in the distance, and the crystal-clear waters down to the pebbles under the rowboat.*

*Lobitos has memories and scars that linger until today. I was badly bitten by a German Shepherd belonging to the neighbors; I tried to take a stick out of his mouth, and the next thing I knew, he had gouged both my legs. It has taken me many years to overcome the fear of big dogs. That notwithstanding, my recollections of this dusty, seaport town are vivid and happy. The childhood friends made there are still in touch with us today.*

*— Rodney*

#

*At about 11 after quite accidentally discovering a huge stuffed bear at the bottom of a trunk, I found out I had a sister who died as a babe. It left me speechless. As instructed by my mother, I remained silent over this traumatic and sad occurrence, placing it in the recesses of my psyche. Even more amazing was that when my siblings and I were alone together, never was the matter broached.*

155

*Subconsciously since then, I have developed a cognizance to all that is unsaid.*

— *Sylvia*

#

As a result of Stephanie's death, we received kind attention from various sources. Ma and Pa in Chile asked us to come to visit them in Llifen, where they were now living after Pa's retirement from Duncan Fox. I'm sure it was the office of Milne & Co in Lima, possibly Tio Fred Milne himself, who agreed to grant me a month's leave of absence so we could accept that kind invitation. The problem of transportation was solved by the kind intervention of Harry Evans, a Chilean employee of Standard Oil in Talara who doubled as Chilean consul there. We had gotten to know him quite well thanks to Joan having been born in Chile. Harry arranged for us to travel together to Valparaiso as non-paying passengers on a Chilean tanker. With all that kindness, we arrived at Llifen and found Ma and Pa in their beautiful home overlooking Lake Ranco.

What a wonderful place and how happy they were. Ma's kidney trouble was apparently not preventing her from taking a very active part in helping Pa keep them self-sufficient during the winter months. That meant making at least one visit to Osorno during the summer when the weather didn't threaten the ferry crossing. The ferry could not be relied on in winter to cross the lake.

I recall one wonderful day when Pa, who was an avid fly fisherman, had Joan, the boys, and me ride upriver on horseback to where he had two boats waiting for the return downriver, which meant a good two hours of fishing. He supplied Clive and Rodney with homemade rods so that they could join in.

The men in charge of the boats were really experts. The current took us downstream so that there was no rowing involved, but they had to keep us in deep water by steering with the oars. There was surprise and jubilation when Clive landed the biggest fish with his homemade rod. This convinced Pa there had been no need to order rods and equipment from Hardy in London when he had been able to make a more efficient—and much less expensive—piece of equipment from the branches of a Chilean tree.

All too soon, it was time to return. We had been told we could use one of the Lobitos Co.'s own tankers that had been undergoing repairs in Valparaiso. But for reasons completely beyond our control, the ship's departure from Valparaiso was delayed, so we were two weeks late in getting back to Lobitos. I could not believe it when the accounting department docked my salary because of that delay in getting back to work. Mr. Linton could have been the only person to give those instructions.

#

Life in Lobitos was pleasant in various ways, and the friends we made there were mostly responsible for that. The Rayner family were the greatest friends of all. I had met Harry Rayner and his wife, Georgina, on my lecture tour. Harry was Lobitos's town manager, so he greeted us when we arrived. They had two daughters the same approximate ages as Clive and Rodney. Our friendship with them lasted beyond us leaving Peru. Sadly, Harry died in Lima while we were there in 1964. And during one of my visits to Lima from Florida in 1999, I had lunch with Georgina and her younger daughter.

There were also enjoyable activities. A group of employees and their wives formed a dramatic society. The mainstay and originator was a young Englishman, John Millea, who had done directing in the army during the war. I was a keen participant in those activities and ended up the lead in various plays the society put on to entertain the oilfield personnel in Talara, Lobitos, and El Alto. I recall taking part in *Rebecca, The Shop at Sly Comer*, and *The Ghost Train*, just to mention a few.

# Chapter Seventeen
# Salaverry Days

*In Salaverry, I lived episodes that can never be forgotten. I still recall the image of my mother—gun in hand—defending all from a villager who had broken into the house and was escaping by way of the roof.*

*As young as I was, I have memories of fearful nights, seeing shadows and countenances through the skylight in my bedroom that left me with an incredible dislike of skylights. A fear I only shed in adulthood.*

*— Sylvia*

#

*Salaverry was nothing more than a tiny fishing village of dilapidated wooden houses, but it had a muelle, or pier, for cargo ships to unload that put it on the map. And we were the only gringo faces in town. As I rode my tricycle along the path from our house, I recall feeling very safe; there was a sense that the whole village was looking out for me.*

*The warehouse next to the company house stored sugar sacks from the Cartavio sugar plantation, destined for* export. *Naturally, it attracted rats, and I recall very well the huge rats that would appear on the back patio and fighting them off with a broomstick.*

*There was a shortage of water, which was supplied to us by rail tanker; I remember being among the villagers as they tried to bring buckets to fill for themselves.*

*My father was constantly out on the freighters that would anchor offshore and have their cargoes barged into port. On many a dark night, these ships were a blaze of light shimmering across the water, lighting the sky, and for us children looking out from the house veranda or from the beach in front, it was both exciting and mysterious.*

*Today, major cruise lines stop now in Salaverry for tourists to visit neighboring Trujillo. It is also the major port for large corporations running mining activities in northern Peru.*

*— Rodney*

#

Prior to the termination of my three-year contract with Lobitos Oilfields, I was summoned by Mr. Linton's office where he asked if I proposed to renew my contract for a further three years.

I was prepared for that question—I was not going to renew my contract—but not for the question he asked after my negative reply.

"Do you have any specific reasons for not wanting to stay with us for another three years?"

After some thought, I made a non-committal reply that I didn't think there was any future in my job, even knowing

Jim Massie was due to retire. That was only one of the reasons. But I did not feel like telling him that the manager of W. R. Grace & Co. in Lima, J.R. Simpson, had personally offered me a job. That was in November 1948.

I asked for a week of local leave from the oilfield to visit the port of Salaverry where I was to be the manager for Grace & Co. I was to meet the incumbent manager and see exactly what Joan, Clive, Rodney, Sylvia, and I were to expect there. After that, I would travel to Lima and meet the management of that Grace office, which was responsible for all Grace interests in Peru. Regrettably, Joan could not accompany me because of the young, so I knew that any decision of mine on that trip would have to receive her blessing. I already had hers regarding my departure from Lobitos Oilfields.

I took the small plane—about 25 passengers—that made the daily Lima-Talara-Lima run and disembarked in Trujillo at about 5 pm. At the airport to meet me were Captain Cherry and his wife Gloria and their friend Ken Gunkel, an engineer employed at the sugar refinery owned by Grace at Cartavio near Trujillo. Salaverry was the port serving the area for almost all the sugar exported from the cane fields owned by Grace. I remember it was a Friday because one of the Grace passenger ships was in port. Salaverry was about 15 km (nine miles) from Trujillo, and we made the journey that evening in record time.

Trujillo, the third-largest city in Peru, was a nice clean place and was a selling point for the job in Salaverry, which was a dirty little port. The fact that we went aboard the Grace Line ship for dinner that evening was also meant to show me how pleasant the nightlife was that went with the job.

During that visit, I found out why the Cherrys so badly wanted me to take the job. Captain Jerry Cherry had been master of a Grace Line vessel and had decided to leave seagoing. Neither he nor his wife spoke Spanish. They did not have many friends in Trujillo; almost all their friends were among the Americans in Cartavio, which was nine miles the other side of Trujillo from Salaverry.

Then there was the matter of water. Salaverry had no fresh water. The company house had been fitted with an underground cement tank big enough to store a week's worth of water that was brought by a truck from Trujillo. The villagers had to buy their water from a vendor who sold it from two large cans carried in by a donkey, one on each side. With regards to electricity, the company house had been fitted with a seven kW generator operated by a four-cylinder Jeep gasoline motor. The generator was started and stopped from switches in the master bedroom alongside the bed and immediately on the other side of a wall that divided the house from the warehouse where the generator was located.

The house and office were adjoining bungalow structures. The manager's office had a door that led to the sitting room of the residence. The other door from the manager's office led to the main office space that accommodated desks for about ten employees. The main office had a public door to the sidewalk, which ran alongside the main railway line between the port and Trujillo.

The residence had three bedrooms, one bathroom, a large dining room, and a large sitting room with a front door that opened onto a roofed balcony with steps down to the sidewalk. The whole construction was of wood as were all the other constructions in the port.

I had very grave misgivings that these salient features of our Salaverry living quarters would not appeal to Joan. I pulled no punches as I described each one. I explained that we would have no problems with expenses for rental or servants since they were taken care of by the company. We were accommodated a cook and one servant, two watchmen, and a chauffeur as well as the vehicle. We would pay for Sylvia's nurse. I told Joan that the salary was superior to what Lobitos was paying me, quite apart from the savings we could expect from daily living costs—we would pay no rent or utility fees. After much talk of pros and cons, we decided to take the job. What really attracted me to take the position was the freedom I was promised to do exactly as I wished, providing it was in the interests of my employers in Lima.

In my own mind, I had decided Salaverry had something I never expected to find in occupations available in those post-war days, namely a Somerset Maughamesque challenge to make more of something that had a lot of nothing by doing what I felt was necessary to achieve results superior to what had been considered adequate, purely of my own initiative. If that sounds unintelligible, I blame you not.

But when we had to leave Salaverry more than three years later, I had a wife and companion who almost shed tears. Without her, I could never have enjoyed that place so much because we both knew that not many couples would have considered taking three young children into a place like Salaverry. Even they recall the happy times spent there with much nostalgia.

#

For the first three months, while getting acquainted with the job, the amenities, and the snags of life, Jerry Cherry and Gloria were still in residence in the Salaverry house. We stayed at the hotel in Trujillo's main square. That hotel was run by the Peruvian Tourist Authority and was comfortable in every way. Somehow Joan managed to keep the children happily occupied while I was away in the port. Jerry provided the transportation for me during that indoctrination period, which thankfully was not unduly protracted; it was clear the Cherrys were keen to start their life in Lima. They had no children so were not in any way hindered in getting their personal things out of the house.

Regarding the work and my responsibilities, there was much that was to be new to me because there was much that was unique in Salaverry when compared to any other job in the world. Joan would find the same in running the household. In the first place, there was no problem in commuting between home and office; in Salaverry, the two were only separated by a door. My bed and my desk were about 30 feet apart.

For obvious reasons, it was necessary to impose some simple rules governing when Daddy was officially at work or at lunch. Once we got settled, the dining room became the schoolroom, which was very convenient when Mummy needed help. Fortunately, that was not very often.

I found out very quickly that little of my time would be spent at my desk—compared with the average manager of any enterprise—because I had to have a say in just about every aspect of the business. W. R. Grace & Co operated a chemical company in the United States as well as one of the most important shipping companies operating from New York and San Francisco. The New York office included two large cruise liners operating to the West Indies. The company offices in Panama, Colombia, Ecuador, Peru, and Chile oversaw the daily operations of large sugarcane fields and textile factories in Peru and Chile as well as insurance companies and metal brokerage in Bolivia. W. R. Grace also operated an airline, Pan American-Grace Airways (Panagra), which shared the New York-to-South America route with Pan-American Airlines. Probably the most important undertaking of the W. R. Grace empire was the Grace Line, which operated more than 20 cargo ships, and they supplied agents in each of the countries their vessels called at.

While the headquarters of W. R. Grace in Peru was their Lima office, the ports in each of those countries had to maintain agencies to deal with the calls of Grace Line vessels. In only one port in Peru did two large interests of the W. R. Grace empire meet and that was in Salaverry. The large Grace sugarcane field was at Cartavio, about 35 miles away, and most of the Grace sugar and molasses were exported from Salaverry to world markets.

It seemed that the management of the Salaverry office had always been put in the hands of foreign—non-

Peruvian—staff. It also seemed very clear that the well-being of the Salaverry inhabitants was dependent on the vagaries of Peruvian politics. Trujillo had always been the center of one of Peru's largest political parties, the APRA, whose fortunes had not been good—or not good enough—to make sure that Salaverry enjoyed electric light and running water. I was told that the electric generator for the port had not been functioning for over a year, ever since the employee in charge took time off to go to see a movie at the Salaverry cinema. He never got to see all of the movie because the power went out. The power failure was caused by that employee sitting in the audience instead of making sure the generator had adequate lubrication. The absence of water was not so easily explained.

The problem of sewage was reasonably well taken care of by alternating the use of two septic tanks. This was necessary when there were high tides or rough seas.

Despite the inadequacies of our living conditions, Joan created happiness where exasperation might have been understandable. She never doubted her capabilities to do a good job as a mother, doctor, and teacher, even while living in the heart of a backward township as the only foreign lady in charge of a household exposed to the possible dangers of violence and robbery. The happiness in our household was an essential ingredient for us to have faced these many challenges.

#

Communication between Salaverry and the outside consisted of a telephone line for the office and one for our house. Visitors had a nasty habit of noting that a call from the Lima headquarters could easily awake me if I was reclining on the sofa in our sitting room. The job was far too interesting for that! Salaverry was not the only port I was responsible for maintaining the efficient operation of Grace Line vessels. To the south was the port of Chimbote, where cargo was offered to our vessels, and north were the ports of Chicama, Pimentel, and Eten, which served the largest sugar fields in South America operated by the German company Gildemeister. All equipment that company ordered from the United States was delivered at those ports by our vessels.

I also had to attend to vessels in those ports, which meant driving considerable distances myself so that the chauffeur could remain at Salaverry for Joan. The whole area is about 300 miles from north to south. The road was good, but I had to rely on the local telephone lines, which were often not immediately at hand. I really could have used a cell phone in those days. With the lack of good telephone service from Salaverry to Lima, I was on my own when immediate action was required. On occasion, I had to phone Joan to deliver messages to the office or to the chief bayman at all hours of the night or day.

The Salaverry manager also served as the agent for Lloyds of London for cargo inspection in the area as well as an honorary consular agent of the United States. Anything connected with an American crewmember's extraordinary activities ashore, or those of visitors and tourists from the United States in northern Peru, was attended to by me. Of course, I could not issue any US government documents, but I was expected to keep the consulate in Lima fully informed.

For instance, when a crew member of a vessel was killed while ashore, I had to be present at the autopsy as a witness. On another occasion, I received a visit from two elderly American tourists who were traveling by road from Alaska and around the continent via Chile and then up the other side back to Mexico and the United States. They had made the big mistake of picking up a roadside hitchhiker of unknown nationality. He had repaid their kindness by helping himself to a lot of their belongings while they were all lodged at the hotel in Trujillo the previous night. I called the local police and of course told the consulate in Lima all about it so they could get the Lima police interested in the case.

Apart from those types of encounters, I was very much aware of the large US colony employed by Grace at their cane fields and sugar refinery in Cartavio. Joan and I made many friends up there, and we arranged social functions during our stay at Salaverry. However, I had a strong feeling that in a large town like Trujillo, there was a greater tie between Peru and the United States among the wealthier citizens of the town. They seemed to ask for more than just recognition on the Fourth of July, and I was happy to get the manager of Cartavio interested in forming a Peruvian-American cultural society. Mr. Rennick was too busy to take part in its formation but was happy to give the idea his blessing.

I contacted the embassy in Lima and soon had a visit from the cultural secretary who insisted that I be the vice president. From then on, we never looked back. Many happy meetings, social events, and international projects for our two countries took place. I was also a member of the Rotary Club in Trujillo, which had been active long before I arrived.

The architecture throughout the village of Salaverry was distinctly Victorian. All buildings were one story and constructed of wood. (I must say that the all-wood buildings and the lack of water did concern me a lot should there be a fire anywhere.) The front of our house faced the sea and the rear of it the homes of Peruvian workmen, of which 90 percent were stevedores, tally clerks, and barge handlers—in other words, the men who worked on the loading and discharge of vessels in the port.

The lack of running water and electricity made residence in Salaverry undesirable for anybody who could afford to live in Trujillo. None of the managers of competing maritime agents lived there, and neither did the port authorities.

It was clear that the relative luxury of the Grace house and my conditions of employment were necessary because it was in the best interest of the company to have the manager living in the port and not six miles away in Trujillo. But to ensure the quality of the water available, it soon became clear that I would have to find an alternative to the existing supply provided by a tank truck from a village near a river. Joe Stansfield, manager of the British railroad that transported sugar from the haciendas to the port, kindly offered to send me a tank car of water from Trujillo each week. I felt certain its origin would be more reliable than the existing source and hastily accepted his kind offer.

When the first train arrived with my water tank, we arranged to unhitch it outside our front door, the nearest place on the railroad line. Everything went well; my hoses connected and the valve was opened. But the delivery seemed to be a signal for a trickle of neighbors to show up with a container, each seeking to somehow get at the water in the truck. The trickle soon became an army, and I had to resort to police protection.

The chief of police, Corporal Caipo, enthusiastically made his presence felt and peace was restored after we had a powwow to settle some sort of *reglamento* covering these weekly water deliveries. Clearly, the most interested party now was me, but it became quite clear that Corporal Caipo and his brave men—or was it *man*—believed their continued protection services entitled them to water as well. I hastily agreed but suggested that since the water was consigned by the railway to me, I could dispose of any water after my own tank was filled and the police's needs fulfilled. When he agreed, I told him that the tank could only be emptied by persons designated by him, since I didn't have any jurisdiction in the port. Nobody laughed much when I said that I nominated him officially as Gunga Din.

I was soon to realize it wasn't water alone that was to seal friendships in Salaverry. I finally got over my discomfort when starting the generator each evening—my house standing out against the darkness of my neighbors' dwellings—when one evening while listening to the radio, the hum of the generator on the other side of our bedroom wall became a thudding, which could only be an overload.

Going outside, I looked down the side street and saw an electric light about a block away. I immediately got the policeman in charge to witness the light and dashed to switch off the suffering generator. That was the last case of wattage theft, and I liked to think that was because thereafter I never refused any reasonable request for a few hours of light and music. I should say that never did I switch off my generator on completion of the time agreed without receiving loud knocks and offended voices a few minutes later, alleging that I had fouled up an enjoyable evening.

#

As I have mentioned, the fear of fire was ever-present in a shantytown with no water like Salaverry. Even if our house was the biggest and most comfortable, it was still constructed of wood. The nightwatchman I employed was a very honest and likable old man, but I know that he was assisted in his physical capabilities by chewing coca leaves. What this did for his quickness of mind, I thankfully never found out.

Grace's Salaverry office was the only one supplied with a revolver. I inspected the firearm when Jerry Cherry introduced it to me. I had doubts about its lethality. It had a cracked mother-of-pearl handle, so I fired it with some trepidation to find out. Only Joan and I knew where it was kept for obvious reasons.

Not long after the Cherrys had left, I was attending to a vessel out in the bay and had told Joan I would undoubtedly be late because the cargo operations would not be completed until the early hours of the morning, so she could turn off the generator when she went to bed. I sailed the vessel at about 1 am then noted with concern that the lights in our house were still on. I dashed ashore as soon as possible and encountered Joan in the kitchen with the revolver in her hand, Maria, the nursemaid, in tears, and the cook standing there fully dressed. Apparently, Maria had seen a man in her room, and he had escaped somehow onto the roof. My attempt at mirth by saying that I now knew why Maria was crying fell on deaf ears.

Joan suggested I make sure that he was no longer in our house or still on the roof, so I climbed onto the roof, revolver in hand. A bright moon was shining, and the stevedores were returning to their homes from the sailed vessel. The sight of me on the roof of our home was too much for the ever-present comedian among them, who shouted that there was room in his house if my wife had thrown me out.

I never doubted that there had been an intruder in our home; that was always a concern about living in the port. I'm glad we never had any serious theft.

#

Grace passenger ships carried more than travelers. Those bound that made port in Guayaquil, Ecuador, would load bananas. The fruit had to be in a certain stage of ripeness on arrival in New York, so the contract for transporting bananas stipulated the vessel needed to be in port within a certain time of the fruit being picked. The bananas were carried in specially prepared decks maintained a few degrees cooler than the atmosphere.

When I arrived in Salaverry, the passenger vessels called every two weeks to load bulk molasses supplied from

Cartavio that was stored in an open reservoir in the port. Pumping the molasses into the ship was done promptly because invariably the bananas had already been loaded when the vessel arrived in Salaverry. What might happen as a result of the delay? Once, New Jersey dockworkers went on strike. The banana-laden vessel sat at anchor unable to berth, and the bananas eventually had to be discharged in semi-liquid form—undoubtedly much to the disgust of the insurance company involved.

Being unsupervised by any senior staff and with labor and materials available at my disposal, I had the great responsibility to consider any action that could enhance the bottom line of whatever account I might render to my superiors in Lima, New York, San Francisco, or New Orleans. The loading operations of the *SS Santa Olivia* at Salaverry produced just such an opportunity. That vessel was scheduled to load a full cargo of bagged sugar, about 6,000 tons, for discharge at Boston. The voyage charter party had given seven days, each of 24 hours, for the whole loading operation.

Only Chimbote had facilities for vessels to berth alongside a wharf. All the other ports, including Salaverry, discharged and loaded cargo while the vessels were at anchor. That cargo was loaded into wooden barges at the pier, and those were towed out to the vessel where they were secured at each hatch. As soon as each barge was empty, it was returned to the pier for reloading. The capacity of each barge was about 50 tons, so in this case, the loading operation for 6,000 toms would need about 120 barge-loads.

The problem was the state of the sea. The coasts of Peru and Chile were famous for heavy swells from the southwest that at times were so severe that the ports had to be closed for as many as three days. Our charter party agreement stipulated that should the port be closed while the *Santa Olivia* was in port, those days of closure would not count. However, I had had the painful experience of vessels working in Peruvian ports on days when the height of the heavy waves was not sufficient to prevent work but still caused the vessel to roll so heavily that there was no way of controlling the drafts of cargo as they were lowered into the holds of the vessel. With bagged sugar, you can imagine what drastic loss could be involved.

Since the rolling was caused by the vessels lying with their bows pointed into the wind rather than the direction the swells came from, something had to be done to keep the vessels with their bows pointing into the swell and not into the wind. Many port managers in Peru and Chile positioned mooring buoys in the bays so the sterns of the vessels could be secured to them in a direction with their bows pointing into the swells. I needed a buoy, heavy chain, and an anchor capable of holding the stern of a vessel in a given heading. Only with that would we be able to avoid disaster.

Well, I had seen a buoy and chain lying abandoned in one of our sheds. Nobody could tell me where it or the chain came from so possession by me seemed all that was needed. Then there was the problem of an anchor. We had no anchor anywhere, but I had seen concrete blocks used for anchors. To make one of those, we had to calculate how big a mold we needed to build that when filled with concrete would weigh about two tons.

My master carpenter sounded like a mine of information on the subject, but before we could start, we had to determine where it should be built, bearing in mind that it had to be on wheels capable of taking two tons safely from our warehouse to the pier about a quarter of a mile away. I obtained permission from the port administrator to use any of his platform rail cars for that operation. What a motley lot of junk. Maintenance seemed to be unknown to those rail cars, but I chose one that appeared to have enjoyed recent attention. The capacity was five tons.

Now here I was with a large, wooden mold filled with cement weighing more than two tons, balancing on one end of a railcar of unknown vintage that was to start a quarter-mile journey over some of the worst rail track I have ever seen. There were about six sets of railway points along the way, any one of which might initiate a jolt that could topple my anchor or cause the collapse of the flatcar's bogies, the framework the wheels were attached to. Either catastrophe would dump two tons-plus of concrete onto the only access to and from the pier. In other words, it would virtually close the port.

About six months ago, I was most interested to see a program on the *Discovery Channel* about the towing of the Troll gas platform from the construction point in a Norwegian fjord to the gas-field in the North Sea. Granted that platform was the largest and tallest structure ever moved anywhere but did I ever get a flashback sitting sweaty-palmed watching how that tow was achieved. It brought back what was at stake in my life and career as my concrete anchor was moved through the port of Salaverry. (Please try to see that video.)

To cut my tale short, we got that anchor onto the deck of a barge in such a position so it could easily be pulled overboard when at the exact position I indicated. The chain was also laid around the gunwale of another barge so that it would follow the anchor without causing damage. How glad I was when that was over and happier still when the loading operation of the *Santa Olivia* went off well as did many, many other operations when we used the buoy to make loading better in every way.

I never regretted taking the post in Salaverry. It seemed that the children enjoyed life there, and Joan did wonders with the Calvert system of home education we had obtained in New York. But when our three-year vacation fell due, we knew we were facing a decision.

# Chapter Eighteen
## Talara

During the English summer of 1952, we took our first home vacation after our first three years with Grace. We had made plans to make Tonbridge our headquarters; Kathleen had bought a small house at Hildenborough after Hamish had died earlier that year.

The most urgent matter was schooling for Clive and Rodney, who were almost ten and eight years old respectively. They'd had kindergarten at Lobitos and then Calvert home system in Salaverry. Now, something more serious was needed, so we looked for a good preparatory school in England.

That decision had been reached after much soul-searching mixed with the need to face facts. Before leaving on vacation, I was given my next assignment in Peru for Grace: opening a new office in the port of Talara, which served the oilfield operated by Standard Oil and was just five miles south of Lobitos Oilfields. It seemed to Joan and me that unless we were posted to a Grace department office in Lima, there would be no possibility of arranging for our sons' schooling in Peru. The distance from Talara to Lima was almost 1,000 miles by car or five hours by plane. We knew nobody well enough in Lima to take charge of their board and lodging and their general well-being.

The only alternative to leaving them in England where we had relatives, was to turn down the job in Talara. The deciding factor was Grace's vacation arrangements for non-Peruvian parents whose children were being educated outside Peru: annual vacations stipulated by Peruvian law of one month accrued a year, could be accumulated over a period of three years to form a three-month vacation abroad every three years. If children were being educated outside Peru, the company would pay for their round-trip travel— in our case London-Peru-London—during each of the two years that the parents received no absence from Peru. In this way, we wouldn't have to ask relatives to look after our children during the English summer vacation months of July and August because they would be with us in Peru. We felt sure Clive and Rodney would look forward to that, to say nothing of our delight in having them with us then.

And so it was that in 1952 we left Clive and Rodney in the care of our kind relatives. Happily, Kathleen lived very close to the preparatory school, Hilden Grange, as did my mother. We felt we had made the right choice although there were many times when we wondered if that was really the case. We know that Clive and Rodney often had their doubts too. But it seemed they were never able to appreciate how thrilling our greetings were to us and how sad our partings each time they left Peru, which they considered their home.

After we had decided on schooling for the boys, we learned that Joan's sister and brother-in-law, Judy and Jack Struthers, and their son, Colin, were returning to England from Chile for good. In 1942, they had both joined up: Judy in the navy as a Wren and Jack in the army. After the war, Jack was employed in Santiago by Imperial Chemical Industries of the UK. It was great news that Jack had been transferred to England by ICI. At least now we would see something of them.

Little did we ever imagine how much we would end up owing them for their kindness in looking after our sons as they grew up. We had some very happy vacations in England thanks to those two dear people who kept us so well informed about their doings and their needs. When they both became unwell, Joan was happy to keep Judy company, and I have some treasured letters from Judy thanking me for letting Joan stay on after I had to return to Peru. How could I ever tell her or Jack that I would always be in their debt, as I am to this day?

#

*As the baby sister who stayed home in Peru, when my dear brothers were left at boarding school in England, the void was ever-present. When I was 11 years old, it was even more poignant when their return visits were greatly treasured by all yet short-lived. When it was time for them to return to England, their departures caused havoc. I always championed any delay tactics whenever possible. I even encouraged Rodney to lock himself up in the bathroom. Very early on, I vowed that I would never send my children away, having witnessed and endured the sorrow and distress of such partings.*

*— Sylvia*

*Being sent off to boarding school in England and left there at such a young age certainly affected me deeply. There are few words to describe the homesickness. It is a sickness, and I recall being paralyzed with sadness once back in England. It's a feeling that I never forgot, repeated over many years as we had to repeatedly say goodbye to family and friends in Peru. Letters were the only form of communication, and I waited patiently for word from my mother who was a prolific writer, always on thin onion skin paper. I sniffed the envelopes when I received them to bring home closer to me. Yes, I became a good letter writer.*

*There are the vivid memories of Talara Airport as a Pangara DC-7B called the Interamericano, came roaring up to the little terminal in clouds of dust and always at midnight. They kept the outboard engines running, lowered a small ladder, and we were hurried out onto the tarmac and bundled out into the plane. My father was allowed to come onboard to buckle us into our seats and kiss us goodbye then quickly disembark. Within a few minutes, we were taxying out and up into the night sky. The tears didn't stop for days.*

*— Rodney*

#

On our return to Peru, I had to relieve the manager of our Callao office while he was on vacation. Callao was the main port in Peru, serving the Lima area. It was a good experience for what was to come later. We could never really convince the friends we made in Lima that we missed life in the provinces of Peru, particularly the north.

I often wondered whether the management of Grace in Peru suspected I had some influence on Standard Oil's management at Talara. Jack Ashcroft, the manager, was a Britisher and only an acquaintance of mine; I would never assume that I could ask favors of him. Captain Joe Scott, the marine superintendent at Talara, was a Canadian and a very friendly type. Jack Spence, Joe's right-hand man, was a charming Canadian I was to become very friendly with. Those three suddenly became employees of Standard Oil; without them, Grace wouldn't have gotten past first base in their endeavors to open up a business in Talara.

Grace had no property in Talara. The vessels of Grace Line only called at that port to pick up passengers. The Pan American-Grace Airways (Panagra) had an office in the town and was probably the Grace organization that reaped the most out of Standard Oil because Talara figured as a regular call for both Lobitos' and Talara's considerable foreign personnel.

My preliminary talks with Grace management in Lima on the commercial and maritime sides were mainly to get an idea why after so many years Grace decided that they needed an office in Talara. It soon became apparent that the commercial activities of Grace & Co. in Peru—*Grace y Cia* in Spanish—would be developed apart from any foreseeable expansion in calls of Grace Line vessels. Grace y Cia had an imposing list it could draw from. The sugar hacienda at Cartavio was second in size only to the Gildemeister hacienda, which was the size of Belgium. The most important by-product of sugar was rum, and Ron

181

Cartavio was one of the more popular brands sold throughout the country. The International Machinery Co, a subsidiary of Grace y Cia, were agents for General Electric appliances and Goodyear tires. The hacienda at Paramonga outside of Lima produced cardboard from bagasse, the by-product of sugar. It had seemed strange to me that the only office with a store to sell these products to the comparatively wealthy communities in the oilfields was in Piura, about 100 miles away from Talara.

I was told the plans now were to build an office and store in the center of Talara; the house for the manager would be built in the residential part, barely half a mile away. I was supplied with a new Chevy Suburban and drove Joan, Sylvia, and our maid, Luisa, with all our goods and chattels from Lima to Talara. We took our time and made the journey in three days.

In the phrase *starting from scratch*, the true meaning of scratch had always puzzled me. Not anymore after our arrival in Talara. That word meant none other than Jack Ashworth, the manager of the International Petroleum Co. I was greeted most affably by Jack, who seemed truly happy that Grace was opening in Talara. I assumed his Lima office would have mentioned my pending arrival to him, and that assumption was correct. He asked how he could help and before long he had the basic list, namely a house and car to rent. Security prompted me to ask for the latter, because of the difficulty I experienced in Lobitos when I tried to drive my own vehicle in the port and refinery areas.

Jack said he was sorry; there was no space in the Punta Arenas area of Talara, which was fully occupied by IPCo employees. But he would be pleased to let me have a small house in the old refinery area rent-free. I knew that would automatically restrict me to driving an IPCo vehicle, so I gratefully accepted his kind offer.

He asked me when I would be independent regarding lodging and transportation. I had to plead ignorance but offered to give him an answer in about a week. Then I asked if I might use a desk in the maritime office. He agreed and asked me to contact Joe Scott.

I thought that was a good start, and before long, I was looking at office sites in the commercial area of Talara. I visited Grana & Montero, the builders and architects hired by Grace to build our house. The first two weeks in Talara were punctuated by several calls to Lima regarding contracts for the buildings. I explained that Jack Ashworth was already asking when I would be independent of IPCo's help.

After three weeks had passed without any news from Grace in Lima regarding the office and house construction, I asked for an interview with Jack Ashworth. To say that I felt uneasy about the lack of any progress to become independent of IPCo's help was a grave understatement, but Jack seemed to understand that it was not my fault. Even so, I had already booked an air passage to Lima, determined to come back with something to report.

I called the manager, Jay Reist, from the hotel as soon as I reached Lima and arranged a meeting for the next day. When we met, I made a point of explaining to Jay how helpful everybody at lPCo in Talara had been, but I was uncomfortable about the progress—or lack thereof—being made in Lima to get our project started. I suspected that IPCo management in Lima might have mentioned our inactivity and asked if it might be possible to arrange a meeting with them before I returned to Talara. I got the impression that Jay really did not know how the arrangements were progressing, so I felt quite justified in overplaying my concern and the importance of obtaining IPCo Lima's full compliance with Grace's plans.

The first thing that happened was that Jay called a meeting with Grana & Montero, the builders in Lima, for that same day. I am certain the ball had been dropped between Grana and Grace. Jay did not want to face IPCo in Lima without recovering the ball. That was duly achieved and then things moved.

I saw the plans for the house and building before I left for Talara, and about a week later, Grana & Montero in Talara had a grip on the matter, and construction started on both projects shortly afterward. The house built for the Grace y Cia manager in Talara was a comparative rarity because it had two stories. Just about every other residential building in the area were bungalows. To go upstairs to bed was a terminology little understood by the local inhabitants. I am sure they built our house that way to provide us with an unusually large garden (yard) area, which was delightful. The area where it was located was not congested since it was further away from the commercial area.

The office building was also more than just a street-level story. It had a mezzanine where I had my private office. Also up there were the accountant and his staff as well as the head salesman. The building's entrance was on the main shopping street and backed on to a pleasant promenade where the smaller stores had their display windows. Altogether, the two buildings did much for the town of Talara, which was built on the shores of one of the driest deserts in the world.

Our life in Talara was made unexpectedly pleasant when Joan and I were made honorary members of the IPCo Club in their Punta Arenas residential community. Invited to take part in all their functions, I was able to indulge in my hobby of amateur theatricals, which had been one of the more pleasant activities in Lobitos' British Club. We were also allowed to purchase our groceries in the IPCo store. Apart from the ease of making lasting friendships with the IPCo staff, it was also great that many of our old friends were still in Lobitos.

Between the two oilfields, I was able to count on clientele for Grace business that didn't conflict with local Peruvian shop-keepers. It was very important that I maintain a good relationship with the locals by buying retail from them because then they bought wholesale from me as Grace manager.

Our most meteoric rise in sales was the line of Goodyear tires, which were supplied from Grace via their merchandizing section of Goodyear products. When I put in for my first tire order, it was based on the recent arrival of the tubeless variety. Many of the interprovince transportation drivers lived in Talara, and the taxis were their own property, so as soon as I knew enough about the details and the advantages of tubeless tires, I arranged demonstrations.

Confident that my campaign would be a success, I placed my first order of tubeless tires before our new office was built, while I was living in the small rent-free house. When the order arrived, I had tires in the backyard, passages, and even in our bathroom for a while. However, sales were brisk, and when I received a telegram from Lima ordering me to send tires to our office in Chiclayo about 250 miles south of Talara because I was overstocked, I was very happy to reply saying that I could not comply with their instructions because I had very few tires left. It was a cliff-hanger for about a week nevertheless.

We held an inauguration party for the house and office. Naturally, the management in Lima figured as guests of honor together with IPCo Talara management and as many local dignitaries as could comfortably fit into our dining and sitting rooms, albeit elbow-to-elbow. After the inauguration, business started to grow as did the shipping agency department. That latter aspect was a surprise. It seemed that some wild-cat drilling by Standard Oil's subsidiaries had shown hopeful signs because I was advised by Grace Line in San Francisco that Richfield Oil of California wanted to start drilling in the Sechura Desert proper; that is, in the area south of Piura. From Talara, the drive to Sechura took about an hour if the ferry over the River Chira was working, otherwise about two hours via Piura.

The first news regarding Richfield Oil in the Sechura indicated that the tonnage involved, coupled with the lack of any road in the desert itself, should be discharged to a beach off the desert and not to the nearest port at Paita. I received news that Richfield Oil vice president would be visiting Peru to see exactly what was involved in discharging about 500 tons of pipe and the machinery required to drill a wildcat well in the northern area of the desert. I would accompany the executive into the desert.

I met the VP, Art Brown, at the Hotel Turista in Piura. He was accompanied by a Mr. Sanchez who was the drilling supervisor for Richfield. Both very affable companions. We traveled by jeep to the desert until the road ran out and we had to follow desert tracks. They had a map marked with the drilling site, and I was pleased to see that it was not far from the beach where I planned to land their material and which was sheltered from the ocean swells.

Once they had located the spot for their camp, we traveled across the desert to the beach where our vessel would discharge to a flat-topped barge. That would beach nearby then the cargo would be dragged off and transported to the camp. What interested me most was the anchorage for the vessel and the beach itself. Was the incline steep or reasonably flat?

Art Brown started to take off his boots to wade in and see for himself. I wanted to do likewise but with my boots on. Beaches in Peru, especially those less frequented, can harbor small, flat fish called weevers that lie just below the sand with part of their dorsal fins exposed. If you step on one of the spiked fins, it injects a venom that causes extreme pain that can last for a couple of weeks. Despite my warning, Art didn't want to wet his boots and sallied forth into the water. He was about ankle-deep when he let out a bellow and came limping back. I told him to sit down while I did the only thing that would ease the pain: suck his big toe where the puncture had been made and spat out whatever came away. That procedure takes place more frequently than people imagine because it is so immediately effective.

The inspection of the beach satisfied me that there would be no major difficulty in landing the cargo there. Undoubtedly, the coastline of Peru would have to be modified slightly by bulldozers to ensure the operation could be done without danger. The bulldozers of course would come with the cargo. Our two days in the desert were interesting ones and supplied us all with good knowledge of what we might expect when the vessels were due.

About a week after my visit to the Sechura desert, I received news that the shipments for Richfield Oil would be coming from New Orleans or Houston on a vessel owned by Lykes Brothers Steamship Company, which was a partner with Grace Line on service to the West Coast of South America from New Orleans and other Gulf of Mexico ports. Their freighters were regular callers in Peru, and many of their masters had become close friends of mine.

Now that I knew the movement was a reality, I had to arrange for a flat barge. The only people with such equipment were my friends the IPCo in Talara, specifically Joe Scott, their marine superintendent. I knew it had been some time since they had needed to use their two large steel barges, so I was certain Joe would be happy to have those expensive items earn their upkeep. Once satisfied they were in good condition, I arranged for them to be at the port of Paita with towboats in ample time before the Lykes's vessel arrived.

The *Gulf Trader* duly arrived at Paita, and all went smoothly, and the operation of discharging from the ship was completed at 10 pm. The customs guards who were to stay aboard until the vessel had completed discharge had traveled to Sechura in the ship, but I was responsible for taking them back to Paita after the vessel had left.

So I bade farewell to the master of the *Gulf Trader* and jumped onto the beach from the launch at about 11 pm. I had given my car keys to the two customs guards who had landed before me and found them sitting in the car snoring. It was a pitch-black night, and the Sechura desert lay before me in that vast blackness. I had hoped that the guards would help me find the way back to Paita and the main road, but they said they had no idea which way to go. So I was on my own.

After starting the car and switching on the headlights, I sat there a moment and considered how I was going to deal with the uncertainty of returning to Paita. The problem was there was no desert surface that clearly indicated how far east I had to travel before turning north toward Paita. Where I was starting from, the sea was behind me to the west and on my left to the north. I needed to travel east straight ahead for a certain distance and then turn north.

If I turned north too soon, I would end up in the sea. If I did not turn north soon enough, I would continue to the center of the desert where nobody I knew had ever been. I knew from my experience in the desert with Art Brown that you had to follow tire tracks, which indicated a surface frequently and recently traveled upon. In broad daylight, those tracks were not too hard to see as long as the wind didn't have time to obliterate them. It was easier in daylight to know where the desert ended and the sea began! Fortunately, I had never heard of any part where the surface was not hard enough to permit traction. I had to be very thankful for that.

I sat there, still pondering. Nothing was visible except my own tracks made when I had arrived early that morning. Sitting behind the wheel of a motionless car was getting me nowhere. The traveling orders issued by myself to myself inaudibly were: *Travel east following the visible tire tracks and then turn north as soon as you see a great quantity of tire tracks heading in that direction.*

I made that journey at a maximum speed of about 20 miles per hour with me bent over the steering wheel glaring at the visible tracks. When they were hard to see, or I saw tracks that appeared to head in any other direction but east, I stopped and studied the visible area granted by my headlights. I remembered once reading about *deafening silence*, and that night I knew exactly what the writer meant. Eventually, tracks heading north became distinctly visible. I turned and followed those tracks. 15 minutes or about five miles later, I stopped and turned off my lights. As my eyes got used to the darkness, I saw a light and heard a dog barking right ahead of me.

I restarted my journey and soon came to a part of the desert where the tracks I was following were joined by a road. Yes, an actual road coming in from my left and slowly turning toward the light and the welcoming dog bark. My passengers soon came to life now that there were signs of civilization. After learning we had arrived at a wildcat rig belonging to IPCo and that there was a road rather than tracks to Paita for the rest of our journey, we gratefully accepted an invitation to have some ice cream before proceeding on our journey.

When I finally returned to my home in Talara, there was another true prayer of thanks as I heard the sound of wings fluttering into the distance.

#

It was inevitable that our stay in Talara would not last longer than three years. But by that time *Grace y Campania* (Talara) was a going concern. Joan and I thoroughly enjoyed those years, and now we were starting yet another chapter.

# Chapter Nineteen
## Lima

On my return to Lima in 1956, I was promoted to manage the main port offices of Grace at Callao, the port for Lima, which was a three-mile car ride away. I was happy with my work there. Life was pleasant in those early days, most particularly because of the friends we made while there. All the ships handled by Grace (Peru) called at Callao, and all the visitors from the US headquarters in New York, San Francisco, and New Orleans made their visits to Callao and Lima before proceeding elsewhere. And it was a certainty that I was going to renew many acquaintances among the many captains who had met me at Lobitos, Salaverry, Talara, or any of the other provincial ports where I might have met them.

Joan and I had no doubts that the hospitality we extended to those captains during their many stays in Lima was truly appreciated because of the kind invitations we received when we had to visit the offices in those three American cities. One of my mental memory exercises to this day is recalling the names of those captains and Grace executives.

#

My time in Peru enabled me to afford Clive and Rodney's education at public schools in England and Sylvia's at San Sylvestre in Lima. My three-month triennial vacations in England provided us with many welcome contacts with relatives, and the boys were able to see us every summer. However, nothing good or bad lasts forever as they say.

It is also true that some changes have more lasting effects than others. One such change was the frequent devaluation of the Peruvian currency, the sol. This had an inevitable effect on businesses deriving incomes from transactions in soles. Above all, it had an inevitable effect on the Peruvian economy. In 1970, 21 years after I started to work in Peru, W. R. Grace & Co. decided to close down all their businesses in South America. Their interests in the United States—Grace Line, Pan-American Grace Airways (Panagra), and their considerable activities in the chemical industry—were unaffected.

In Peru, Grace y Cia's vice president in charge of the marine department was a Peruvian named Leonardo Pratt. We'd been close friends for many years, and he'd had a meteoric career in the company. I wasn't surprised when W. R. Grace offered him the agency for Grace Line ships should he wish to form a company to take over that business. Nor was it a surprise that he agreed to form that company then offer me a post as his assistant with the same salary and conditions, including my annual bonus in US dollars. So I stayed on as Leonardo Pratt's right-hand man.

Then in 1976, the surprises started.

The first was a friendly conversation with Leonardo where he said he was very sorry to tell me that the bonus due to me would not be in dollars but in sols at the official rate of exchange. I hesitated before accepting that, making it clear in the politest way possible that it was not in accordance with our gentleman's agreement blah, blah, blah. What I could not say was that I suspected that my interests would be in greater danger the following year when the rate of exchange would mean fewer dollars for me. That line of conversation would only lead to revealing my suspicions that Leonardo was systematically decreasing the value of the job he had originally offered to make room for a line of younger Pratts who would expect their father to find positions for them. Claudio, at the head of the line, had just finished his education in the United States, and behind him stood Justin, Michael, and Louis.

The next year was a difficult one. There is only one book of rules that lays down how to face responsibilities. Those rules are the only ones of any value and are well known to everybody. The problem I faced was that my responsibility was suddenly being rewritten by the person who was paying me, but the person who was paying me was not fulfilling the responsibilities for which *he* was getting paid and would eventually suffer as a result of the rewritten rules being applied to me.

In short, I discovered that certain employees in Callao who were close friends of Leonardo Pratt were in charge of the cargo operations of Grace Line vessels. On two occasions, I went down to the port when gangs were at supper break, 11 pm to midnight. Both times the employees were not back by midnight and work had not started. The first time, I warned the person involved. The second time, I told Leonardo that I wanted him fired, and I did so. I also told Leonardo that those employees were keys to a good operation when I was not around. He did not appear enthusiastic about my solution.

To cut a sad story as short as possible, I was determined to look for another job as it seemed the dice were stacked against me in the one I had.

It was at this stage in my life that I first had cause to worry about my mother's welfare. She was living in a small house at Hildenborough in Kent, which my sister had bought after her husband, Hamish, died. Kathleen had gone to Scotland, which left my mother very much on her own. This worried me because it didn't appear Kathleen would return south in the near future. I asked friends in London shipping circles about jobs in England and one day, I received news of a presidency opening for an outfit called International Cargo Handling Care Association.

The company was comprised of representatives from shipping companies who were interviewing candidates in London. It was a long shot for me because one of the requirements was to speak French fluently. So though I had a knowledge of French, I certainly had not been fluent in that language since I was ten years old when we had to speak French for two months while governesses from Paris lived with us at Crabtree Furlong.

My concerns regarding continued work in Peru had become greater. Successive governments seemed to have lost interest in striving for a successful national future and replaced it with greater interest to ensure personal economic stability. Military takeovers were more likely to take place than democratic elections.

In that atmosphere, I was again to hear the fluttering of wings. This time, they accompanied a telephone call from William Hagan who was vice president of Lykes Lines Agency Co, a subsidiary of Lykes Brothers Steamship Company of New Orleans. He wanted to know if I would be interested in filling the post of owner's representative in South America. We had met when Grace Line sold their services to Prudential Lines earlier that year, thus leaving the services of that Line free for all comers.

I was pleased to accept the job, as you can imagine. Though it was a relief to be working for an employer whose feelings and purse were not subjected to nepotism, I was sorry that it separated both Joan and me from the Pratt family. However, I felt sure that our paths were very likely to meet again if my office remained in Peru.

#

My duties as owner's representative were to oversee the agents already named in South America and the sub-agents in each country. Lykes Brothers only had services from New Orleans to Panama and to countries on the West Coast of South America, but it had shared that revenue with Grace Line when it was in operation. Now that Grace Line had disappeared, Lykes could compete for any and all cargoes between the United States and the West Coast of South America.

It became apparent very soon that my first duties would be to revise all the agency agreements that the Grace Line had entered into with their agents in South America to ensure that they all understood that Lykes had no connection anymore with Grace Line or any other Line that had taken Grace Line's place.

Bill Hagan, the vice president I reported to, called the agency managers in South America to a meeting in New Orleans shortly after I started my new duties. All the managers of the various agents in Panama, Ecuador, Bolivia, Peru, and Chile—with their assistants—turned up, and it gave me a great chance to meet some old faces from the Grace Line past as well as new ones. That of course included the Pratt son who had taken over from me in Peru. It was natural they would want to carry on as Lykes's agents in Peru, but I could see a conflict of interest rearing its ugly head; they already represented the line that had purchased the Grace Line New York and San Francisco services.

The most important duty of an agent in South America is freight solicitation. That was why the freight salesmen of each agency accompanied the manager of each agent to the meeting in New Orleans. On the capacity and efficiency of the salesmen depended the main value or otherwise of the agency to each line. My office in Peru was in a shopping center between Lima and Callao. It was here that I was able to count on the services of Miss Carmen Arias who had originally worked for W. R. Grace in Lima and later in Callao. She was the person who assisted me in organizing work in Callao and the outports of Peru when Grace Lines services were the busiest.

I had devised a colorful board showing all the Peruvian ports with small cardboard vessels of different colors. One of her duties was to maintain updates as vessels entered

Peruvian waters. I felt very happy that I had someone with previous experience of that kind since I could foresee that much of my time would be taken up traveling to the other countries served by Lykes Bros on the West Coast of South America.

It wasn't long before Lykes's management in New Orleans determined that I needed a full-time assistant. Bill Hagan decided we should run a job listing in the main London dailies and that I should go to London and interview the best candidates. So I duly traveled and interviewed eight candidates on the first day and four on the second. That evening, I called Bill Hagan and told him my impressions of those interviewed and felt there was a good prospect of finding the right person. But he soon called back and told me that the chairman of the board, James Amoss, had a friend he wanted me to interview in New Orleans.

So I flew back, interviewed the friend, and reported to Mr. Amoss that his candidate was superlative. He was an ex-Grace Line officer married to a Chilean lady. (Didn't they already have one of those?) This was surely a superlative combination. Herman Fritzke was a charming, easy-going man about 45 years of age but had little experience with the sort of work he would have to do and no capacity for absorbing the Spanish language despite his wife being Chilean American. She had given up the struggle to teach her husband elementary Spanish, so I suggested that he be employed on a trial basis and subject himself to the Berlitz School of Languages for subsequent evaluation.

Back at Callao, I was immersed in the work, which I much enjoyed. It did indeed involve a lot of travel, and Bill Hagan was keen to learn about the ports and agencies on the western side of South America. As a Lykes employee, he headed up a parent company of the Lykes organization called Lykes Lines Agencies Company with a head office in New Orleans and Agencies in London, Antwerp, Hamburg, Marseilles, and Genoa. This was up until Lykes Brothers Steamship Company decided to extend its services to South America alone rather than in partnership with Grace Line. Hagan had never been to South America before so I accompanied him on his travels. He was aware that Joan was left alone while I was with him, and he soon invited her to accompany him to Chile where he knew she had friends.

He asked me to arrange a schedule for the three of us, which I did. First by air from Lima to Tacna where we were met by a Chilean taxi driver who took us by road to Arica where we spent two days. Then to Antofagasta for a three-day stay. Then to Chanaral for two days. Then to Valparaiso where we spent a week after dispatching our taxi. We then went by air to Talcahuano and Concepcion, and after three days, returned to Santiago. A week later, we flew back to Lima.

I often wonder who enjoyed that trip most. It must surely have been a tie. Bill Hagan reminisced about it 25 years later and told me he'd like to do it again!

# Chapter Twenty
## Panama

In 1983, my life changed considerably. One morning about 8 am when our handyman, Juan, was outside cleaning the car, three men approached, pointed a revolver at him, and told him to enter the house through the patio toward the kitchen entrance. He obeyed. He was about to enter the kitchen when Joan also did so from the dining room. She was shocked to see the three men and the pistol. They told her to keep quiet and return to the sitting room.

I had just come down the stairs and was entering the sitting room when I saw the men, Joan, and Juan. I do not recall the sequence of events exactly, but the men started to rip the electrical cords off the lamps with the idea of using them to tie us up. Juan assumed a macho attitude and started to resist. I shouted to him to desist because the only pistol belonged to the other side. Joan expressed concern about the damage to the lamps, and the men assured her that she would not be harmed.

I was asked where the wall safe was. Before I showed them, they tied Juan up and Joan's ankles. After I returned with them from the empty wall safe in the passage, they tied me up. The men were very well dressed. The boss told me that they were ex-police officers who were dissatisfied with the government. They made no suggestion as to what I could do about that.

While we lay on the floor, they asked a series of questions. They told Juan to give them the key to the large car, and before Luisa arrived, they were gone, car and all— but not before first warning us that we should not report the matter to the police lest we want further assaults on our household.

The first outcome was that I got my car back. It was found undamaged a couple of miles away. It seemed that the vehicle was what they first wanted. However, their assault on my household concerned Lykes Brothers in New Orleans. They were aware of personnel being kidnapped for large ransoms. They asked me to consider moving my office to Panama. I think that a Mr. Hobson had once to make a choice like this, or so I have heard. So we prepared to move.

#

*I was present during this house invasion. The sense of fear, vulnerability, loyalty, and shock were overwhelming then, and they have never been forgotten. It changed so much for me, but it also impacted the children remaining in Peru any longer.*

*The resilience of my parents on that occasion was in play and came from the strength they encountered in the war years. Indelibly etched in my memory was my father's steely, unwavering countenance while face down on the floor, instructing our chauffeur to desist from fighting on the family's behalf and my mother undauntedly rationalizing with the intruders. But most mercifully, as a result of much pleading by me, my young children were untouched as they were sleeping upstairs at the time.*

— Sylvia

#

For a gringo leaving a South American republic where they've lived for 40 years, it is not a simple procedure of just paying the balance due in income taxes since the last annual payment. It turned into a presentation of all receipts since I paid the first year's taxes, which in my case were those Lobitos Oilfields should have paid when my contract with them terminated in 1949. I will not describe the frustration I felt during that period until I finally got my permit to leave.

Needless to say, I was deeply concerned about how Joan viewed my transfer and the radical change it created in our lives. When Bill Hagan first suggested the move, I told him I would have to consult with Joan. After all, there was little doubt that she would sorely miss her friends in Lima; I knew so well that she was not one of those people who could quickly replace friendships of such long-standing, particularly in a different country where the conditions of my work, according to Hagan, would have a different pattern. When he said I would be traveling more, that raised my first concern about Joan's happiness in Panama.

One of my main responsibilities as owner's representative was checking the accounts rendered by sub-agents in each country for services rendered to each vessel in each port. I have already mentioned that another responsibility was soliciting transportation of cargoes to and from each country by Lykes's vessels. Clearly, the sub-agent was responsible for supplying efficient and sufficient employees for solicitation.

My office hired an adequate number of employees—whose salaries were paid by Lykes, New Orleans—to check the accounts of each sub-agent. I had two employees who did nothing except check vessel accounts. They were Peruvians who handled all matters with sub-agents in Spanish. Discrepancies noted by them were passed to my secretary who dealt with each of the sub-agents by letter or by telephone in either Spanish or English with New Orleans.

I explained to Bill Hagan that I would leave the two employees who were checking accounts in Lima, and if necessary my secretary, Carmen, as well. But I needed someone in Panama as a secretary who was experienced enough to deal with account discrepancies while I was traveling.

Bill asked if the employees in Lima needed supervision of their daily duties.

I explained that any deterioration in their work would soon be noted, though I had great confidence in them since they had been working for me for several years already.

He suggested that Carmen should also be transferred to Panama, providing that Panamanian law permitted it and that my office there should also get a copy of each vessel account so that she could check the discrepancies as they were found or consulted on.

So it was that after nearly 38 years in Peru, Joan and I left to work in Panama. We were both happy to be free of worrying about any further terrorist attacks on our household. I know that Joan was very happy about that. In those days, the Panama Canal was still under the control of the United States. I had asked Bill to accompany us as we made the rounds of available living quarters since Lykes covered that expense. The very comfortable apartment we chose was not in the Panama Canal Zone, but it had a wonderful view of the Pacific Ocean.

During the two years that we were there, I did a lot of traveling both alone and accompanied. There seemed always to be someone who found it easier to travel from New Orleans to Panama where the currency was pegged to the US dollar, and the language and life, in general, were so much like that at home. Peru was in a different category indeed, with so much done over the telephone where Lykes's business was concerned.

There was one employee, however, who liked to travel regardless of the country involved. That was my boss, William Hagan. All he needed was my company and a good reason to undertake our journeys. During those two years, we changed all our sub-agents in Panama, Ecuador, Peru, and Chile.

I am sure you can appreciate the traumatic effect these changes had on me. During the years that I had represented Grace Line in Peru, because I was an employee of Grace Line's parent company W. R. Grace, I was the sub-agent in Peru. As such, I dealt directly with the captains of the Grace Line and Lykes Lines vessels calling at Peruvian ports and also with the managers of Grace Line and Lykes's vessels in all countries where their vessels called. All of a sudden,

Grace Line was gone, and only Lykes was left to compete with any line that had bought out Grace Line's services.

Several of the original purchasers opted out, but right from the start, the ex-Grace Line agents expected that they would continue to represent Lykes even though the new owners of the Grace Line services were now competing with Lykes. I knew that Hagan would never accept that state of affairs and offered each of the agents in each South American country the choice of either representing Lykes or its competitors, not both. Bang went a lot of friendships for me because among those who applied to act as Lykes's agents were countrymen of mine who were managing the steamship businesses of the Pacific Steam Navigation Co. that employed me before the war and where I had risen to second officer, as well as those who expected me to use any influence I had to overlook them as competitors and demonstrate friendship of long-standing.

The procedures in changing our sub-agents in South America involved many meetings then drawing up the new contracts once the decision was made to either represent us exclusively or not at all. The discussion with Leonardo Pratt for the future representation of Lykes was the only one that worried me. Leonardo had separated from his wife of many years and remarried, acquiring new family responsibilities and four more children. At the meeting held in the boardroom of the Lykes office in New Orleans, the oldest son from the first marriage, a naval officer who would soon be in line for the rank of admiral, and the next oldest son who had replaced me, decided to accompany their father. Their intention, presumably, was ensuring that their mother would not be negatively impacted by any arrangements made regarding the representation of Lykes's interests. They were clearly aware that the second Mrs. Pratt was going to be present at the meeting, and as a shareholder, she was representing the future interests of herself and her young children.

Indeed, there was a moment before the meeting when I had to explain to Lykes's management who it was that we were dealing with in the Pratt organization.

The outcome was that Lykes could not accept the representation of their interests by the L. Pratt Agency while that agency represented Lykes's competitors. That same evening, Lykes invited the Pratt family to dinner, and as we walked out of the restaurant afterward, I was surprised when Leonardo asked me if I would pass by his hotel that evening before I went to mine. Bill, who had earlier offered to drop me off at my hotel, agreed that I should go alone to see what Leonardo wished to talk about.

I still do not know why Leonardo wanted to speak to me. We sat and had a drink and it seemed that he was waiting for me to say something. Or maybe he had decided not to say whatever it was he had planned to.

Ultimately, we gave out business in Peru and Chile to German agencies. There was never any doubt in my mind that they were better organized than the offices of the Pacific Steam Navigation Company in either of those countries. It was good to feel confident that our choices were justified.

# Chapter Twenty-One
# Carmen

No account of my life would be complete without mentioning my secretary, Carmen Arias. That dear lady came into my life in 1957 as my secretary when I was appointed to the Grace y Cia office in Lima. She had just completed her secretarial training at the age of 25 and was one of the few employees who could do bilingual work in English and Spanish as a shorthand typist.

Leonardo Pratt had just been named head of the maritime department of Grace y Cia, Lima and wanted to be certain that letter-writing in English or Spanish, which was one of my duties, would be properly done by my secretary. When I was appointed manager of the Callao office, I left Carmen in Lima. But later in the 1970s when Leonardo Pratt concentrated the marine office in Callao, Carmen was again available because Leonardo had plans to replace me with his son Claudio.

When I eventually landed at Lykes Brothers, Carmen was working for Leonardo. I imagined that she would want to carry on in that position; however, when she asked me if her salary could be guaranteed if she came to work for Lykes as my secretary, I was very happy to tell her that was no problem. She was ready to leave Pratt, and over time, events permanently tied Carmen Arias to me and my family. The first of those was that terrorist attack on my home in San Isidro.

On the heels of that attack, I moved offices to Panama and asked Carmen if she would be agreeable to also move her place of abode to Panama. She agreed. The move meant Joan was leaving behind all her friends, but she found a new, sincere friend in Carmen.

After I retired from Lykes in 1986, Joan and I left Panama and settled in Naples, Florida. Carmen returned to Peru and resumed working for Lykes Brothers accounting office in Lima, which remained open while there were ships making calls at South American ports. Also, there were the two Peruvian employees I had taken on when joining Lykes in 1976, who had done that repetitive work so well for so long. I was very glad they were still earning a livelihood.

During one of her vacations, Carmen came to spend two weeks with us here in Naples. I know that Joan had missed her companionship ever since we left Panama, and she welcomed Carmen's help in the kitchen now. Carmen told us then that she had received a notice from Lykes that the office in Lima would be closed in about six months.

When Joan underwent surgery in 1994, she sent a card to Carmen telling her that she would be very welcome to stay here if she had any spare time. Joan told me that she was worried about me driving alone to the hospital and back in the evenings. The hospital was in North Naples about six miles away. Carmen did come back for a while in 1995 but had to leave after a few days to close the office, so she was in Lima when Joan died on January 24, 1996.

But Carmen has been keeping me company ever since then. It is not easy to describe the comfort I get from Carmen when she recalls memories of Joan and the way she showed Carmen how to do things in the kitchen. She still does that, so my comfort is on-going. I only hope that our association has been as comforting to Carmen as it has been to me.

I do not know what I would have done without Carmen's company for the last five years. It just isn't possible for family members to be at the beck and call of the aged. Life has enough difficulties in raising a family, getting a job, and listening to parents, without being responsible for knowing what ails the aged at any moment in their precarious lives. I can never repay the help and understanding that I have received from my children. I know that whatever happens, they will never expect me to give them more than heartfelt thanks in payment. I believe that they will be the first ones to also feel gratitude toward Carmen.

# Chapter Twenty-Two
# Retirement

*Assisting my father and mother secure residency in the United States was a logical step after Latin America. They settled in Naples, Florida. It was both touching and saddening to see that my father, up to the age of 80, was forced to work, having no pension after such an incredibly busy life in Latin America. And yet I was always impressed and proud of his cheerful demeanor, first in a department store and then in the Naples Courts. He never complained.*

*I had connected to my father's naval career and love of the sea. It was at that point in both our lives that I acquired a small sailing boat. From that point on, he taught me more than I could ever learn from any sailing school. My love of sailing continues today; when I'm out there on the seas, I feel him and feel I am part of his legacy.*

*— Rodney*

#

Trying to write something about my retirement, I have wondered what makes it so difficult, yet at the same time so important. I suppose that for a start, it's rather a long time for someone who has been active to suddenly be faced with forced inactivity—ten years without the need to be at a given place at a given time to undertake duties affecting other people.

When Joan and I came to Naples, Florida, I very soon began to feel like a fish out of water. Looking for somewhere to live made me come face-to-face with the realization that I would never have enough money to buy an apartment unless we were prepared to die within a year—or two at most. So we were faced with renting somewhere within our means; that is to say, putting up with accommodations which made only the most meager hospitality possible for any family who might visit us. Without income, there seemed to be a very limited horizon. I'm sure that Joan felt the same although she never said anything to me, bless her.

I have written how happy my working days in England and South America were and how happy I have been while writing about them. I am not going to depress anyone who reads what I have written by dwelling any longer on the sadness of unprepared inactivity. Before leaving the subject, I wish to express deep gratitude to my darling wife for being so thoughtful toward me throughout the time that we shared those difficult days, to those members of my family and friends who have been so kind in helping us weather them, and to the Good Lord who has given me the health to make some amends for my shortsightedness.

It was not very long before I told Joan I would look for work that I figured I was physically able to do and that wouldn't mean long hours away from home. I answered one ad for work in shipping and other transportation that turned out to be in a tourist concern where my presence in the evenings and possibly at weekends would almost certainly be needed.

Finally, I walked into Luria's—a store dealing in jewelry, cameras, and high-quality gifts—about a half-mile away from our apartment and filled out an application then and there. I was soon contacted.

"Can you come in tomorrow?"

I said I couldn't, "But yes, the day after."

I met some very nice people while I was with Luria. Regrettably, the hours of standing around and the need to occasionally work weekends forced me to look elsewhere for other work. One day, I applied to a listing from the local courthouse for an interpreter and received an immediate reply in the affirmative.

For a while, I assisted a Mrs. Miller, a Cuban lady married to a heart specialist. She wanted to give up her position, which was why they were looking for someone else. I took over within four months and stayed there till I reached my eightieth birthday. I am sure that I could have stayed on, but Joan's health worried me, and I decided that she also needed a rest from the cooking chores my job was making necessary.

My duties as a court interpreter included making sure there were interpreters in court for whatever languages other than Spanish were needed and whenever more than one Spanish interpreter was needed. This brought me into contact with people living in Naples who spoke Haitian and French as well as those who spoke Spanish. The most important work for me was in court. Every Thursday morning, there was a court in Immokalee, a small town about seven miles from Naples, and interpreting was very frequently required in the nearby jail. Whenever needed, I also did interpreting for law firms in Naples and the surrounding area, provided it did not conflict with my duties in the courts.

It's strange how hard it is for me to recall the dates when things happened ever since my retirement to Naples. I never had that difficulty when writing about things that happened over 50 years ago. I believe one of the reasons for this sudden difficulty is there has been a sameness about those events. For instance, my visits to Peru have always been made before the drab winters set in on that country during the months of June, July, and August when I traveled to the U.K, where summer was being enjoyed. Each year has been punctuated with those absences from Naples where summer is something to be avoided if possible.

# Epilogue

Merriam-Webster's unabridged dictionary defines epilogue as *the final part that serves typically to round out or complete the design of a nondramatic literary work; a speech often in verse addressed to the audience by one or more of the actors at the end of a play.*

I have written no literary work, but since someone of great literary importance did once state that the world is a stage, I'm going to borrow that heading.

Yes, I have come pretty close to the end of my act on this stage, and I dedicate these few lines not to an audience but to my fellow actors—my family—who have accompanied me so lovingly to this point. Only they will find anything of interest in what I have written.

I woke up a few nights ago and started to think about how I would close these writings, which deal with my personal life. I then recalled someone saying or writing that life is just a game. The more I thought about that, the more I thought how closely that description fitted my personal life.

Games are played for enjoyment, but they are played to strict rules that determine who wins and who loses. How did that fit into the description of my life as a game? Do I have a trophy to show that I have been a winner? No, if trophies are measured by personal wealth, I am indeed a sorry loser.

How much I have wished that I could leave something as a gift to all of you. Before falling asleep again, my guardian angel, whose flapping wings have so often indicated his presence, again appeared in my consciousness. The person who started the life is a game theory went on to say that it does not really matter who wins or who loses because the most important thing is how the game is played. My consciousness again said that I did not have to worry because my failures had all been forgiven, and there were signs I had played the game well.

I leave you here with some unsolicited testimonials as to how I've been judged by others who accompanied me during the less pleasant stages in the game of life. I do not think that my story would be complete without them. I wonder if there is any life lived these chapter days without some regrets. I hope that I may be forgiven for presenting these testimonials with a little pride to compensate for those regrets. Much love to you all.

Father, Papi, Dablee
Naples, Florida
May 23, 2003

#

*Coming to terms with his retirement after a very active, interesting, dynamic, and fulfilling career was not easy for my father. As so often occurs, it was not a good fit for a man who had not developed any hobbies and interests, exacerbated by having lost so many meaningful friends and a lack of funds. However, his account in this memoir affirms for me—in no uncertain terms—that he played the game well.*

*— Sylvia*

Goodwin as a cadet on the *HMS Conway* Training Ship.

*HMS Conway* Corvette Naval Training Ship founded in 1859 on which Goodwin received officer training.

Richard serving aboard *RV Reina del Pacifico* of PSNC line
from Liverpool to Valparaiso where he met Joan as a passenger.

MV Reina del Pacifico of the Pacific Steam Navigation
Company built in 1930 sailed between Liverpool and the Pacific
coast of South America until 1939 and then served as a
troopship from 1939 until 1946.

Richard and Joan recently engaged in Chile.

Joan's wartime voyage from Chile to UK to marry Richard
aboard steamship *R.M.S. Samaria* of White Star Cunard line.

Richard and Joan married in Chalfont St Giles,
Buckinghamshire, UK at the height of the war.

*HMS Borde* with 400 ton electromagnet, Goodwin's first experimental minesweeping assignment.

Cmdr. Goodwin served on *HMS Whitehaven* Bangor Class minesweeper on longest sweep of the war through Mediterranean – 1942.

Cmdr. Goodwin outside Buckingham Palace with wife and mother after awarded the Distinguished Service Cross medal for gallantry from King George VI.